UPGRADING YOUR MAC ILLUSTRATED

Written by
Tom Negrino

UPGRADING YOUR MAC ILLUSTRATED

Library of Congress Catalog No.: 94-68567

ISBN: 1-56529-917-5

97 96 95 94   4 3 2 1

Interpretation of the printing code: the rightmost double-digit number is the year of the book's printing; the rightmost single-digit number, the number of the book's printing. For example, a printing code of 94-1 shows that the first printing of the book occurred in 1994.

Screen reproductions in this book were created using Capture from Mainstay, Camarillo, CA.

Publisher: David P. Ewing

Associate Publisher: Corinne Walls

Publishing Director: Brad R. Koch

Managing Editor: Anne Owen

Product Marketing Manager: Greg Wiegand

Composed in *New Baskerville* and *MCPdigital* by Que Corporation

Credits

Publishing Manager

Thomas H. Bennett

Acquisitions Editor

Nancy Stevenson

Product Director

Jim Minatel

Production Editor

Chris Nelson

Editors

Danielle Bird
Nicole Rodandello

Technical Editor

Carrie Obenchain

Acquisitions Assistant

Ruth Slates

Editorial Assistant

Theresa Mathias

Book Designer

Amy Peppler-Adams

Cover Designers

Dan Armstrong
Amy Peppler-Adams

Production Team

Accent Technical Communications

Julie Kirkendall
Richard T. Whitney

Macmillan Computer Publishing

Stephen Adams
Becky Beheler
Claudia Bell
Cameron Booker
Karen Dodson
DiMonique Ford
Jason Hand
Clint Lahnen
Nanci Sears Perry
Dennis Sheehan
Kris Simmons
Craig Small
Mary Beth Wakefield

Indexer

Michael Hughes

About the Author

Tom Negrino is a writer and Macintosh consultant, who has worked with the Macintosh since its introduction in 1984. He is a Contributing Editor to *Macworld* magazine, and he holds the same position at *Digital Video* magazine. He has also written for the late *MacGuide* and *MacComputing* magazines. He's served as both moderator and panelist on the conference faculty at the Macworld Exposition trade shows in San Francisco and Boston. Mr. Negrino has been a member of the Los Angeles Macintosh Group's Board of Directors for the past several years.

Prior to 1984, he worked in the film business as a videotape editor and production coordinator for industrial films, music videos, and commercials. He currently lives in the Los Angeles area with his wife.

Acknowledgments

The author would like to acknowledge the help and support of the following people, without whom this book would not have been possible. Thanks, folks.

Rocky Pyle, service manager, and Mike Descher, owner, at Mac Universe in Tarzana, CA, for technical support extraordinaire.

Paul Mandel, co-owner of APS Technologies, for lending me the help of APS's excellent tech support department. Thanks to Doc, too.

The ever-patient Carol Person at *Macworld* magazine, who let me slide on her deadlines so that I could make this one.

The Que folks, especially Nancy Stevenson, Jim Minatel, Chris Nelson, and Ruth Slates. They made my first solo book project surprisingly painless.

And finally, for moral support and encouragement above and beyond the call of duty, I'd like to thank my wife, Betty Negrino.

Que thanks Accent Technical Communications for its assistance in getting this book done on schedule.

Trademark Acknowledgments

Contents at a Glance

TABLE OF CONTENTS

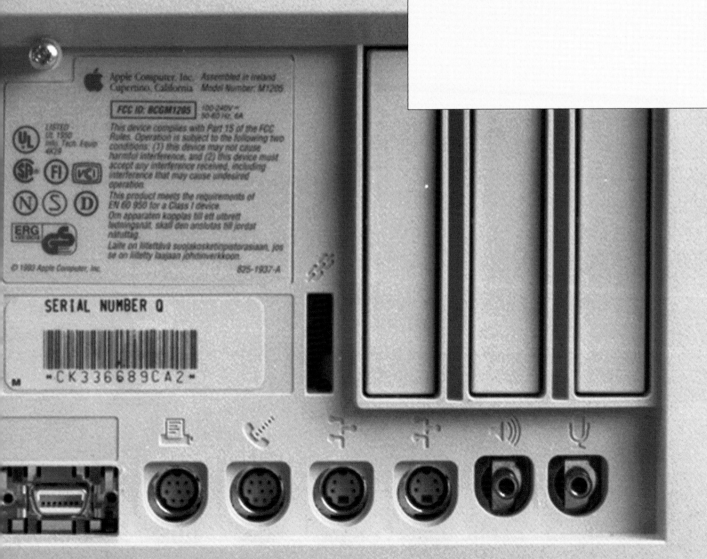

CHAPTER

1

Why Upgrade?

Why Should You Upgrade?

You should upgrade if you like the computer you have, but just want *more*. More memory. More disk space. More speed. More capability. Upgrade if you want more, but you're not ready to jump to a new computer. You can get better performance by investing just a little money.

What Can Be Upgraded?

Virtually any aspect of your Macintosh can be upgraded, from internal parts, such as memory and the microprocessor, to external peripherals, such as a printer, scanner, or modem. The table below lists some representative Mac models and the upgrade options available.

Upgrade options for some Macs.

Macintosh Model*	RAM	VRAM	Monitors and Video Cards	Accelerator Cards	Cache Cards	Hard Drive	Internal CD-ROM
SE/30	•	•	•	•		•	
Classic II	•			•		•	
IIsi	•		•	•		•	
LC, LC II, LC III	•	•	•	•		•	
IIci	•		•	•	•	•	
Quadra 605	•	•	•			•	
Centris/ Quadra 610	•	•	•	•		•	•
Centris/ Quadra 650	•	•	•	•		•	•
Quadra 800	•	•	•	•		•	•
Power Mac 6100, 7100	•	• (7100 only)	•		•	•	•
Power Mac 8100	•	•	•		• (beyond 256 Kb)	•	•

*CPUs listed in ascending order of processor speed.

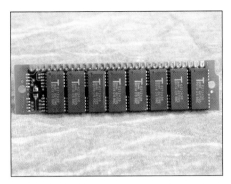

RAM (p. 58).

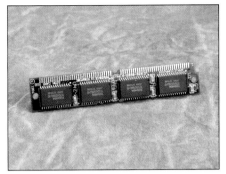

VRAM (p. 77).

Accelerator cards (p 36).

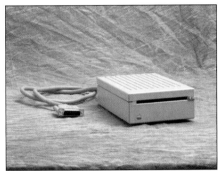

External floppy disk drive (p. 88).

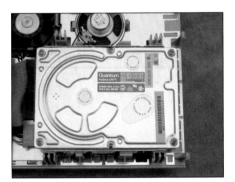

Internal hard drive (p. 94).

Internal CD-ROM drive (p. 107).

Monitor (p. 80).

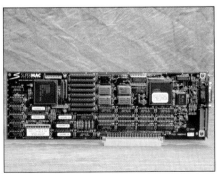

Video card (p. 80).

In addition to the upgrades above, all Macs can benefit from these other upgrades:

- **External SCSI devices.** Hard drives, tape drives, CD-ROM drives, removable-cartridge drives, scanners.

External hard drive (p. 101).

External tape drive (p. 120).

External CD-ROM drive (p. 112).

Removable-cartridge drive (p. 123).

Scanner (p. 132).

- **Printers.** Inkjet, laser (PostScript or QuickDraw), color.

Inkjet printer (p. 145).

Laser printer (p. 146).

- **Modems**

Modem (p. 148).

- **Externally powered speakers**

External speakers (p. 154).

• **Input devices.** Trackballs, keyboards.

 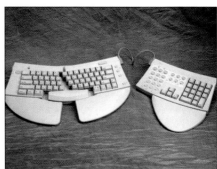

Trackball (p. 164).   *Keyboard (p. 162).*

IS UPGRADING COST EFFECTIVE?

Besides making technical sense, upgrades must also pass the test of practicality. It doesn't always make economic sense to pour lots of money into your existing Mac to bring it up to the performance level of a newer Macintosh. Let's look at a few examples.

RAM UPGRADES

RAM upgrades usually make sense, especially if you've got a fairly recent Mac or want to increase your RAM by a modest amount. Let's say that you have a Centris 650, which came with 8 Mb of RAM, and now you want more RAM so that you can work with more programs open at the same time. You can add one 8 Mb RAM SIMM, doubling your memory, for about $290. Because the Centris 650 uses the newer 72-pin SIMMs, you'll be able to use the RAM when you upgrade to a Power Macintosh next year.

On the other hand, what if you have a Mac IIci with 5 Mb of RAM, and you want to jump up to 20 Mb? You'll need to buy four 4 Mb, 30-pin SIMMs, at a total cost of about $520. This is where you start to ask yourself, "How much is my Mac worth used?" As of the summer of 1994, a IIci with 5 Mb of RAM and an 80 Mb hard disk was selling for about $700 on the used market. It makes little sense to invest close to the IIci's worth in extra RAM. Rather than have a total investment of $1,200 in the IIci, it would be smarter, in a case like this, to sell the IIci and buy a new Quadra 630 or Power Macintosh 6100.

To find used prices on Macintoshes, check the charts in most issues of *Macworld*, *MacUser*, or *MacWEEK*. The Classified areas of online services such as America Online also are good places to price used equipment.

HARD DRIVES

A bigger hard drive nearly always makes good economic sense. If you swap your internal 80 Mb drive for a 500 Mb drive, for example, you can always put your old 80 Mb drive on the shelf and reinstall it in your old Mac when you get ready to sell that machine and buy a new one. Then put the 500 Mb drive in your new Mac.

ACCELERATOR CARDS

This kind of upgrade needs careful thought. If you have a 68030-based Macintosh, a 68040 accelerator usually makes sense only if you already have a lot of RAM. Let's think about that IIci again, but assume that it already has 20 Mb of RAM, bought years ago. Putting in a 33 MHz 68040 accelerator card, at a cost of about $800, makes sense because a comparable new Quadra 650 with 20 Mb of RAM costs almost $2,300.

For an example of an accelerator card upgrade that doesn't work out economically, consider this scenario. You've got an LC II and you want to double your speed. You buy a 68040 accelerator for $800. That gets the LC up to about the speed of a Quadra 605. But you can buy a brand-new Quadra 605 for only $900, so the accelerator is a waste of money.

EXTERNAL PERIPHERALS

Adding any external peripheral, from hard drives to modems, makes economic sense because you can always transfer the peripheral to a newer Macintosh when you step up to a new computer.

Chapter

2

Before You Get Started

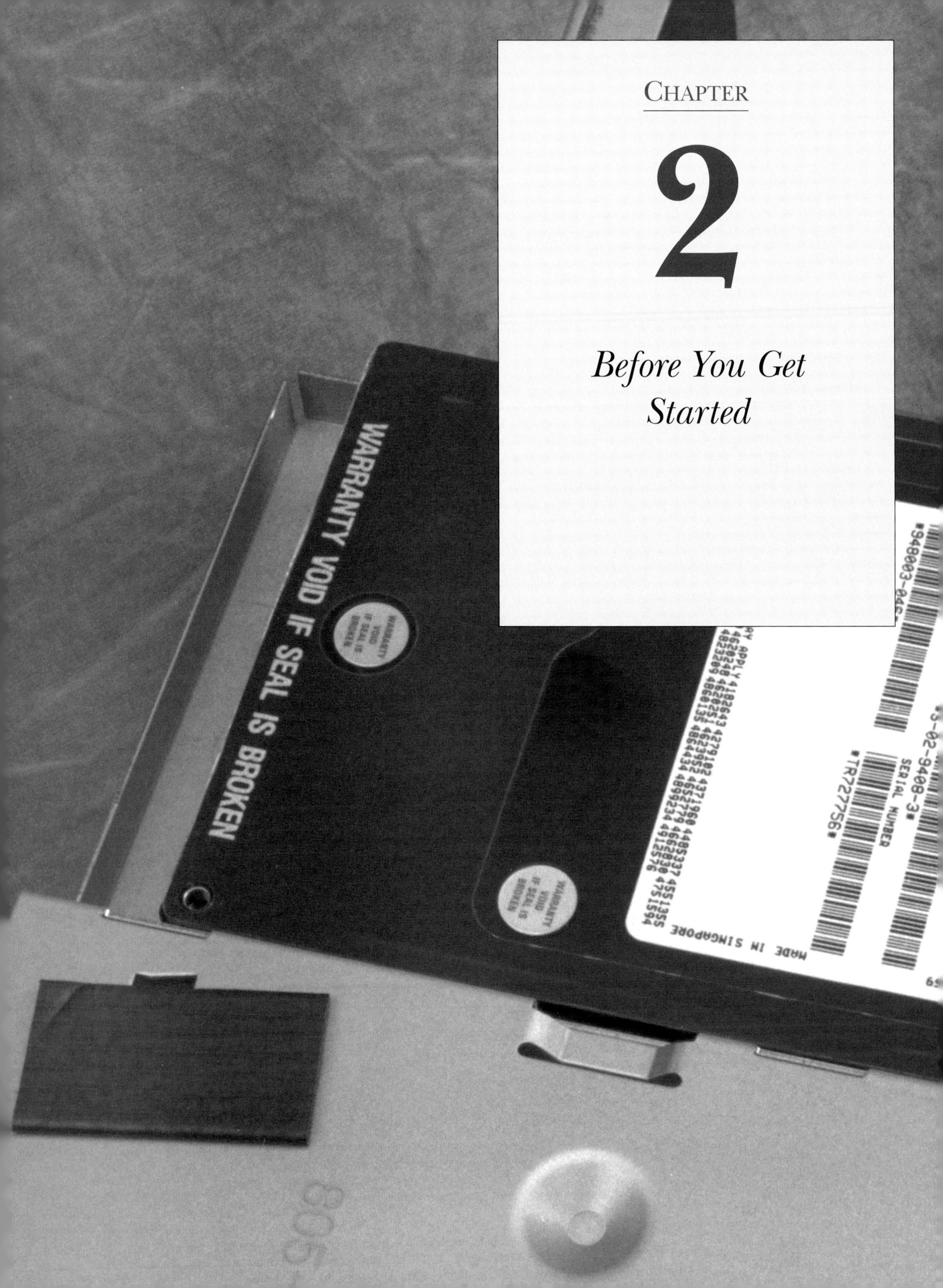

CREATE AN EMERGENCY STARTUP DISK

Before you start any upgrade, it's a good idea to have an emergency floppy disk on hand which you can use to start up your machine. Such a disk came with your Macintosh; it's called the Disk Tools disk.

The Disk Tools floppy disk.

You should also create an emergency startup disk with the Installer program that comes on your System Software disks. Do this by running the System Software Installer for the type of Macintosh you have. You'll find the Installer on the Install Me First disk. Install a "Minimum" System (for your specific Macintosh) on an 1.4 Mb floppy disk. You'll find this in the "Custom" options. By making an emergency startup disk ahead of time, you'll be better prepared if your Mac has problems. If by some chance you don't have your System disks anymore, it's a very good idea to obtain a set from your local dealer.

BACK UP BEFORE YOU UPGRADE

It's important to back up your hard disk before you upgrade your computer. It's possible, though unlikely, that you'll damage the computer during the upgrade process. You'll want to make a backup copy of your precious data before you go poking around.

BACKUP MEDIA

The easiest way to back up is to copy all your data onto 1.4 Mb HD floppy disks. This works great if you back up no more than 40 Mb. When you back up more than that, it gets tedious, not to mention impractical. If you have more than 40 Mb of data to back up, you should back up to a tape drive, a SyQuest cartridge, or another hard disk. See whether you can borrow a friend's external drive for an afternoon, and then back up your data.

BACKUP PROGRAMS

You may think that all you need to do to back up one hard drive onto another is to drag one hard disk's icon onto the other. Think again. This method does not work as well as you would hope. Sometimes files and folders aren't copied correctly by the Finder, and copying a lot of files with the Finder is very slow. You're better off if you invest in a backup program.

One of the best programs for backing up a hard disk, whether it be to floppies, SyQuest cartridges, or other hard disks, is DiskFit Pro from Dantz Development. Easy to use and fast, DiskFit Pro is about $75 via mail order, and your local computer stores probably carry it.

Other decent backup programs come as part of utilities packages. Symantec's Norton Utilities for Macintosh has Norton Backup, and Central Point Software's MacTools package has CP Backup.

If you choose to back up to tape, the best choice is Retrospect 2.1, also from Dantz. This premiere backup program is bundled with the vast majority of Mac tape drives sold in the US.

BACKING UP TO FLOPPY DISKS

Backing up your hard drive to floppies using a backup program isn't difficult. Here's an example with DiskFit Pro.

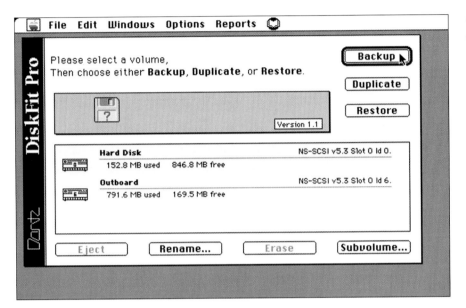

Choosing the hard disk for backup.

1 Double-click the DiskFit Pro icon to start the program. When the DiskFit Pro screen appears, select the hard disk that you want to back up and click the Backup button.

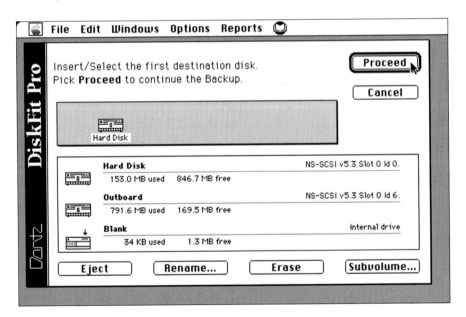

Choosing the back-up destination.

2 Insert a blank floppy disk. If the disk needs to be initialized, DiskFit Pro will do so automatically. Select the floppy disk in the DiskFit Pro window and click the Proceed button. If you have an external SyQuest drive, you can instead select it and use the SyQuest drive as your backup medium.

3 DiskFit Pro backs up data onto the floppy disk; as each disk fills, DiskFit Pro ejects it and asks for another one.

HOW TO DO A CLEAN REINSTALL OF YOUR SYSTEM SOFTWARE

On occasion, your Mac won't boot because the System Software has become corrupted. Simply reinstalling with the Installer disks that came with your Mac won't do the trick, because there's something in your System Folder that is waiting to bite you. The solution is to do a "clean install," which creates a new System Folder on your hard disk. Here's how to do it:

1 First you must disable your existing System Folder. Do this by moving the Finder and renaming the System Folder. Open your hard disk's icon and locate the System Folder.

2 Create a new folder outside the System Folder and name it Old Finder.

3 Open the System Folder.

The Finder from the old copy of the system is in the Old Finder folder.

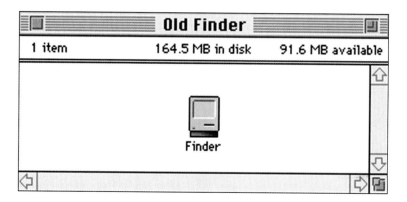

4 Locate the Finder within the System Folder and drag it into the Old Finder folder.

5 Close the System Folder's window and rename the folder. (You can name this anything you want except System Folder.) Close all windows on your desktop.

The old System Folder here has been renamed Storage.

6 Shut down your Macintosh.

7 Insert the Install Me First floppy disk (it's part of your System Software disk set) and restart the computer.

The Apple Installer screen for System 7.1.

8 When the Welcome to the Apple Installer message appears, click OK.

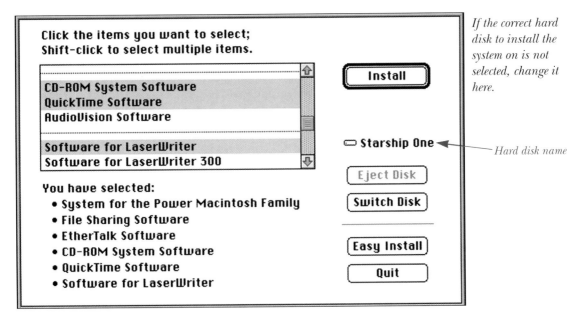

If the correct hard disk to install the system on is not selected, change it here.

— *Hard disk name*

9 Be sure the correct hard disk is selected for the installation procedure (click Switch Disk if necessary). Click the Install button.

10 When the installation is finished, the Macintosh will restart.

11 You can now reinstall the nonstandard items, such as fonts, extensions, control panels, and so on, by dragging them from the old System Folder (named Old System Folder) to the new System Folder. Be aware that reinstalling items from the old System Folder into the new System Folder may reintroduce corrupted files.

Selected extensions to move to the new System Folder.

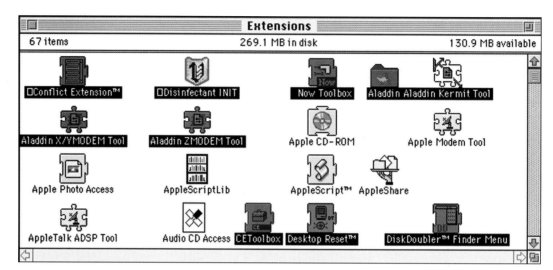

12 After you are done moving files from the old System Folder to the new one, restart your Macintosh.

13 Verify that your applications perform normally. If they do not, refer to the program's manual or contact the software manufacturer. When you're sure the Mac is working correctly, drag Old System Folder to the Trash, and choose Empty the Trash from the Special menu.

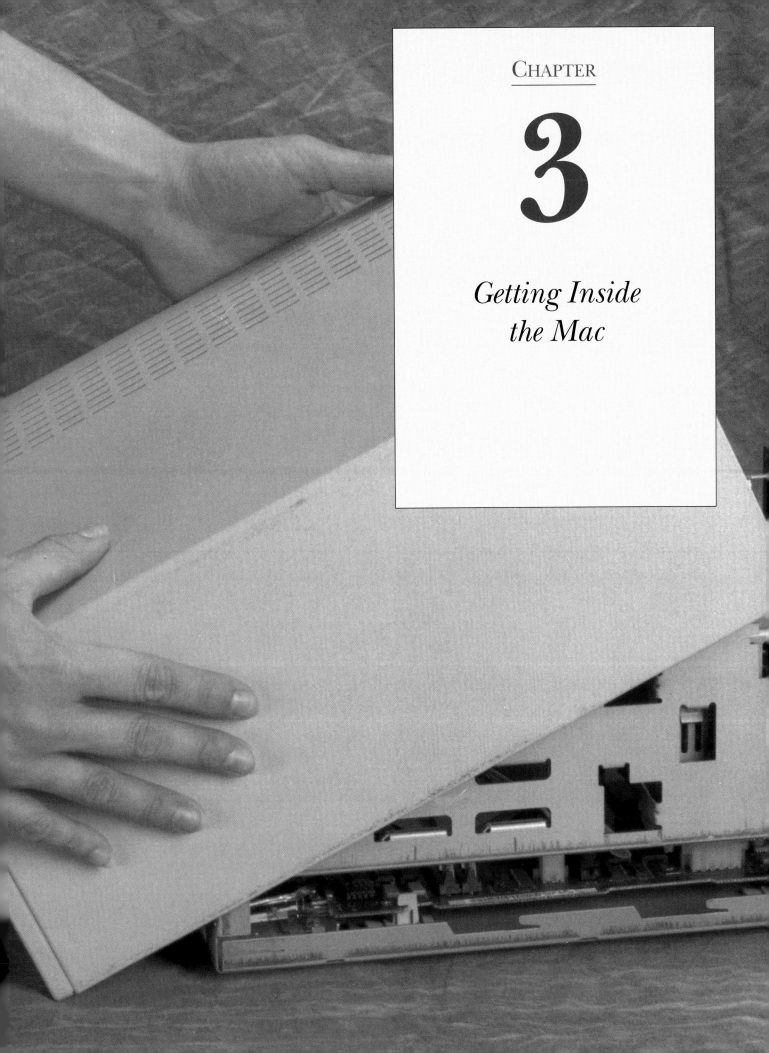

CHAPTER

3

Getting Inside
the Mac

OPENING YOUR MACINTOSH

This chapter is the most important in the whole book. Refer to this chapter to find out what tools you need; to open your Macintosh for internal upgrades; to learn the functions of the expansion ports on the back of your Mac; to identify parts on the Mac's motherboard; and to learn about important safety precautions.

TOOLS OF THE TRADE

You don't need to make a large investment in tools to work on your Mac. Usually all that you need are medium-size (#2) Phillips and flat-blade screwdrivers. It's also helpful to have a long set of tweezers; tweezers are handy when you drop a screw into a hard-to-reach crevice inside your machine.

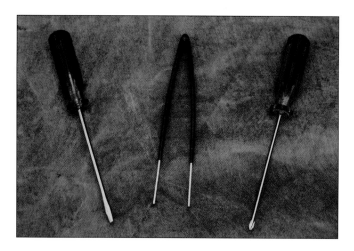

A flat-blade screwdriver, tweezers, and a Phillips screwdriver.

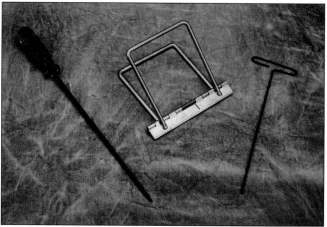

The Mac Cracking kit (for compact Macs only). The Torx T-15 screwdriver is on the left; the case spreader is in the middle. The tool on the right is a less-expensive version of the Torx screwdriver.

If you'll be working on a compact Macintosh (the SE, SE/30, Classic, Classic II, or Performa 200), you'll also need the Mac Cracking kit. This consists of a long Torx T-15 screwdriver and a tool for spreading the case halves apart. You can find this kit through the larger mail order companies, such as MacConnection or MacWarehouse, or through some of the better stocked computer dealers and superstores.

In addition to these tools that you absolutely must have, a pair of small needle-nose pliers is good to have. If you want to be even better prepared, go to an electronics store and pick up a small computer toolkit. These all-in-one kits typically cost under $30 and include tweezers, nut drivers, and several types of screwdrivers.

A typical computer toolkit.

SAFETY FIRST

Upgrading your Mac is a fairly safe process, but you should be aware of some issues. To upgrade safely and successfully, follow these simple guidelines:

- Work slowly and carefully. There's never a good reason to be in a rush when you're working inside a computer.

- Working inside a computer can seem complicated, scary, and frustrating for a nontechnical installer. If you find yourself getting frustrated at any time, take a break. Even if you're not upset, a work break every 15 minutes or so is still a good idea.

- Before you begin work, remove all rings, watches, and other jewelry from your hands or wrists.

- Notice the order in which you perform operations. Associate parts with their origins inside the computer. Make notes, if necessary, as you disassemble things.

- Keep a small dish or container handy to hold loose screws that you've removed from the Mac. If you don't, I guarantee that a screw will roll away, and you'll end up on your knees looking for it.

- Make sure that you follow the procedures, described in the step-by-step instructions throughout this book, to ground yourself from static electricity. When working on a computer, avoid polyester clothing, as it holds static electricity very well. Besides, you'll look better in natural fibers.

- Always unplug the computer when instructed to do so.

- The square silver box at the back of the computer's chassis is the power supply. This plugs into the motherboard—the large green circuit board with computer chips on it—via a connector on the bottom of the power supply. The power supply is self-contained, and you cannot fix it if it goes bad; all you can do is replace it with a new unit. Because they can hold an electrical charge for a long time, even after the computer is unplugged, never try to open a power supply. You could be in for a shocking—and dangerous—surprise.

- Read the step-by-step instructions for a particular operation all the way through before you begin the operation.

WHICH MACS ARE SHOWN IN THIS BOOK?

There are so many different Macintosh models that it would be prohibitive (not to mention redundant!) to shoot step-by-step upgrading sequences for every model. We show you four models that are representative of the entire Macintosh line, past and present. Because upgrading on one model is often very similar to upgrading on another model, you'll be able to use the step-by-step instructions we provide to upgrade a wide variety of Mac models. We picked the following four models (although you will see a few other models as needed to illustrate special procedures): the Classic II, the LC II, the Centris 650, and the Quadra 840AV.

MACINTOSH CLASSIC II

The Classic II uses the traditional compact Macintosh case. It has a built-in 9-inch monochrome monitor and room for one internal third-height hard drive and one floppy drive. Similar Macintosh models include the Macintosh SE, SE/30, Classic, Color Classic, and Performa 200.

The Macintosh Classic II.

Monochrome monitor

Floppy drive slot

The rear of the Classic II.

Cooling fan opening

Power switch

AC power connector

MACINTOSH LC II

The "LC" stands for *low-cost*, and the LC II was the second of the computers from Apple to use the so-called "pizza box" style case. Based on the original LC, the LC II has a 68030 microprocessor and built-in color video. You can add a wide variety of monitors to the LC-class machines. These machines have one expansion slot. Macs similar to the LC II include the LC, LC III, Quadra 605, and the Performa 400, 405, 410, 430, 450, 460, 466, 467, and 476. Generally speaking, upgrading tasks on any of these Macs are similar, though not exactly identical to upgrading the LC II.

The Macintosh LC II.

Rear of the LC II.

Case latches

AC power connector

Power switch

Expansion ports

MACINTOSH CENTRIS 650

The Centris 650 is built on the chassis used by Apple for its mainstream business computers. It has a 25 MHz 68040 microprocessor and three NuBus
expansion slots. The Centris 650 has one internal floppy drive and one internal 3.5-inch hard drive bay. There's also a 5.25-inch drive bay for an optional
CD-ROM or SyQuest drive. In late 1993, the Centris 650 received an internal
revision with a faster (33 MHz) 68040 processor and a name change; it's now
the Quadra 650. Similar Macs with the same case design include the
Macintosh IIvx, IIvi, and the Power Macintosh 7100.

*The Macintosh
Centris 650.*

*Rear panel of the
Centris 650.*

*Monitor AC
connector*

NuBus slots

AC power connector

MACINTOSH QUADRA 840AV

The Quadra 840AV is designed with the "mini-tower" chassis first introduced with the Quadra 800. The 840AV is the fastest 68040-based Mac, with a 40 MHz processor. It has three NuBus expansion slots and room for three internal SCSI devices, plus a floppy disk drive. The "AV" in the computer's name means *audiovisual*, and the 840AV can take in video and stereo audio signals, recording those signals to disk. Similar Macs include the Quadra 800 and the Power Macintosh 8100.

The Macintosh Quadra 840AV.

Rear panel of the 840AV.

Monitor AC connector

AC power connector

Video ports

NuBus slots

EXPANSION PORTS AHOY

You need to become familiar with the expansion ports on the back of your Mac. These ports are where you plug in cables for networks, modems, printers, external hard drives, scanners, external speakers, and microphones. Here's a rundown of each type of port, and what it does. Not all Macs have every type of port.

EXPANSION PORTS ON MACINTOSHES.

Port	Icon	What It Connects
ADB (Apple Desktop Bus)		Mouse, keyboards, and graphics tablets
Ethernet		Ethernet networks
Floppy		External floppy disk drives
Modem		Serial port for modems
Monitor		Monitors
Printer		Serial port for printers, built-in LocalTalk
S-Video In		S-Video input (AV Macs only)
S-Video Out		S-Video output (AV Macs only)
SCSI		External SCSI devices (hard drives, CD-ROM drives, removable-media drives, scanners, printers)
Sound In		Microphones
Sound Out		External speakers, headphones
Video In		Composite video input (AV Macs only)
Video Out		Composite video output (AV Macs only)

Expansion ports for a Classic II.

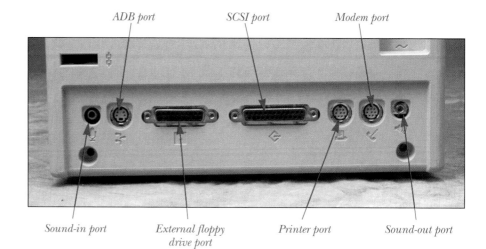

ADB port   SCSI port   Modem port

Sound-in port   External floppy drive port   Printer port   Sound-out port

Expansion ports on the back of an LC II.

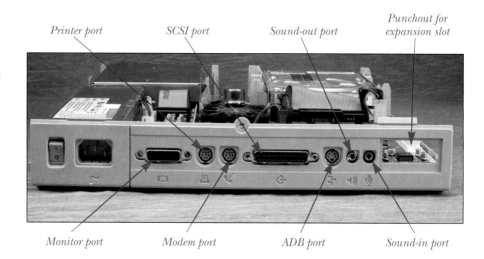

Printer port   SCSI port   Sound-out port   Punchout for expansion slot

Monitor port   Modem port   ADB port   Sound-in port

Expansion ports on the back of a Centris 650.

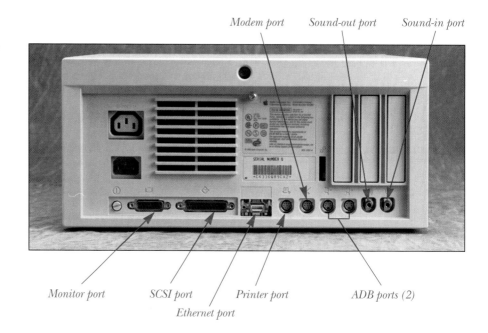

Modem port   Sound-out port   Sound-in port

Monitor port   SCSI port   Printer port   ADB ports (2)

Ethernet port

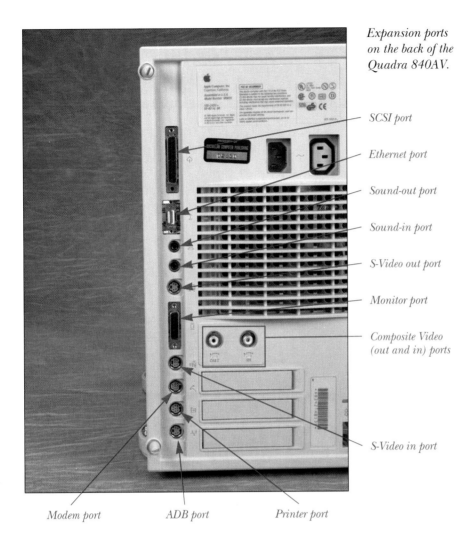

Expansion ports on the back of the Quadra 840AV.

SCSI port

Ethernet port

Sound-out port

Sound-in port

S-Video out port

Monitor port

Composite Video (out and in) ports

S-Video in port

Modem port

ADB port

Printer port

OPENING THE MACS: STEP BY STEP

Follow these steps to open each type of Macintosh. For the Classic II, you'll need the Mac Cracking kit; for all Macs, you'll need a flat-blade or Phillips screwdriver.

CAUTION: Static electricity from your body or clothing can damage the sensitive electronic parts inside your computer, such as RAM and processors. Whenever you work inside your Mac, leave it plugged in and touch the power supply to discharge the static. This will discharge the static through the power cord, which will not damage your Mac. After you discharge the static, you should unplug the Mac; you don't want the computer plugged in while you are taking it apart. Take care not to build up static while working. Shuffling your feet on carpet and brushing your hair are common generators of static.

For further safety, you can use a grounding strap. This strap keeps you grounded at all times, which prevents you from building up static.

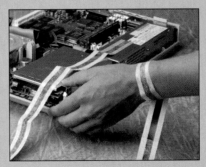

One end of the grounding strap goes around your wrist, the other attaches to the power supply.

OPENING THE MACINTOSH CLASSIC II

1 Unplug the power cord and any other cables attached to the back of your Macintosh.

Screw locations

Removing the two top Torx screws.

Removing the two bottom Torx screws.

2 Using the long-handled Torx T-15 screwdriver, unscrew the two screws inside the case handle.

3 Next, unscrew the two Torx screws at the bottom of the case.

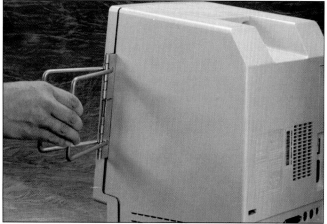

Cracking the case sections apart.

Removing the rear case.

4 Insert the case-cracking tool in the crevice between the two case sections and spread the sections apart. If you don't have a case-cracking tool, you can often pull the two case halves apart by hand. You also can use small, spring-loaded wood clamps in lieu of a case-cracking tool.

5 Pull the rear case section away from the front section. You may find it easier to do if you set the Mac face down.

Floppy drive   Hard drive   Cathode-ray tube (CRT)   Motherboard   Power supply

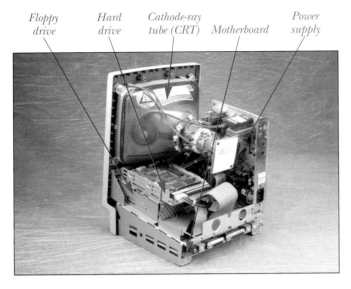

The Classic II with the case removed.

Beware the high-voltage CRT.

6 Set the Mac upright to work on it. Make sure to avoid touching the cathode-ray tube (CRT), as it can hold an electrical charge, even when the Macintosh is unplugged.

OPENING THE MACINTOSH LC II

1 Unplug any cables attached to the back of your Macintosh.

Removing security screw.

Lifting the case release latches.

2 In the middle of the rear panel, above the SCSI port, is a case security screw. Remove it with the Phillips screwdriver.

3 Lift up on the case release latches on either side of the back of the case and gently lift the lid from back to front.

Lifting the LC II's lid.

Removing the LC II's lid.

4 When you lift the lid enough, it will release in the front. Lift it completely off and set the lid aside.

Inside the LC II.

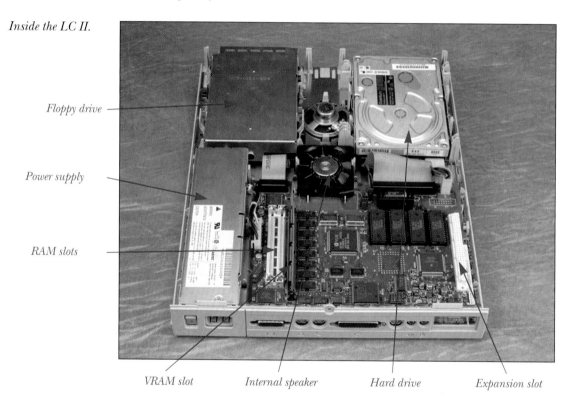

Floppy drive

Power supply

RAM slots

VRAM slot　　　Internal speaker　　　Hard drive　　　Expansion slot

OPENING THE MACINTOSH CENTRIS 650

1 Unplug any cables attached to the back of your Macintosh.

Loosening the case screw.

Loosening the case.

2 In the top of the rear panel, above the SCSI port, is a case security screw recessed into the bezel. Loosen it with the flat-blade screwdriver; it will not come out. Don't mistake this screw with the Phillips screw beneath it.

3 Pull the case towards you about an inch.

Pulling the case off.

4 Gently pull the case up and off the computer.

*Front view of the
Centris 650 with
the case removed.*

Power supply

Hard drive

Speaker

5.25-inch drive bay   *Floppy drive*

NuBus slots   *RAM slots*

*Side view of the
Centris 650 with
the case removed.*

Power supply

5 Take a minute to familiarize yourself with the interior of your Mac
before you proceed.

OPENING THE MACINTOSH QUADRA 840AV

1 Unplug any cables attached to the back of your Macintosh.

Loosening the case screws with the screwdriver.

Loosening the case screws with your fingers.

2 With the flat-blade screwdriver, loosen the four screws on the back of the Quadra 840AV. The screws will not come all the way out.

3 Once the screws are loose, unscrew them the rest of the way with your fingers.

Lifting the case off.

4 Slide the cover forward about an inch, and lift it from the computer.

*The interior of the
Quadra 840AV.*

CD-ROM drive —

Power supply —

Drive bays —

NuBus slots —

5 Take a minute to familiarize yourself with the interior of your Mac before you proceed.

PUTTING THE CASE BACK ON

If you paid attention when you removed the cover, you'll have no problems reinstalling it. All you need to do is reverse your steps:

Centris 650 Tip: *To make sure you've seated the cover properly, check the two buttons at the left bottom front of the cover. These are called the reset and interrupt switches. If you've got the cover on correctly, these switches should protrude slightly from the front of the cover. If they don't, or if there's visible space between the front of the cover and the two buttons, slide the cover off and reseat it.*

1 Replace the cover, making sure that it slides onto the case properly.

2 Secure the cover with the same screws that you removed or loosened when you removed the cover. You didn't lose any of the screws, did you?

3 Attach any cables (monitor, serial, sound, Ethernet, ADB, or SCSI) that you had previously disconnected from the back of the Macintosh.

4 Plug the power cable into the power socket on the Mac and into the wall outlet or your surge protector.

TESTING YOUR SYSTEM

Test your system by turning it on and starting it up as usual. Fully test everything related to whatever you upgraded to make sure that the upgrade is in good working order.

If your computer doesn't work properly, retrace your steps. You'll often find that you left one small step undone.

Here are some specific possible problems and solutions.

Problem	Solution
You turn on the Mac, but nothing happens.	Is the Mac's power plugged in? Is the monitor plugged into the Mac?
When the Mac starts up, you hear several odd tones instead of the usual startup sound, and the screen has an icon of a sad Mac on it.	You probably just installed a memory upgrade. Check to see that the memory modules are seated properly and that you have the correct number of SIMMs in the memory slots. If that doesn't work, replace the SIMMs with new ones.
The Mac starts fine, but it doesn't see any external SCSI devices.	You have a problem with SCSI termination or SCSI address. Check Chapter 9 for help with SCSI problems.
You start your Mac, and after a brief delay you get the blinking disk icon.	Start up from a floppy disk, and reinstall your System Software.

TOURING THE MOTHERBOARDS

A computer's main circuit board holds the microprocessor, the RAM, the expansion slots (if any), and many other components. This main circuit board is often referred to as the *motherboard* (also sometimes called the *logic board*). When you upgrade your Mac's internal components, you'll often have to locate one part or another. Here's a guide to finding the parts you'll need on each Mac's motherboard.

MACINTOSH CLASSIC II MOTHERBOARD

The Macintosh Classic II motherboard.

Expansion ports

SCSI cable socket

Floppy drive cable socket

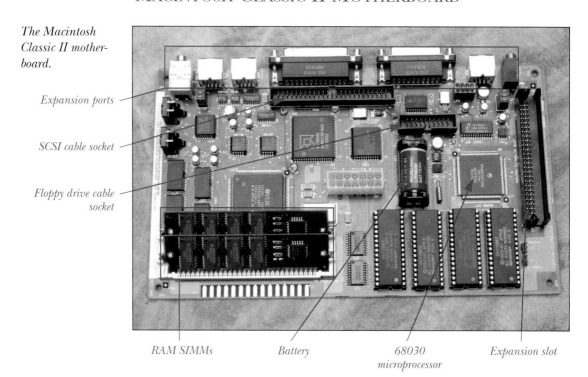

RAM SIMMs   *Battery*   *68030 microprocessor*   *Expansion slot*

MACINTOSH LC II MOTHERBOARD

The Macintosh LC II motherboard.

RAM SIMM slots

VRAM slot

Expansion ports

68030 microprocessor

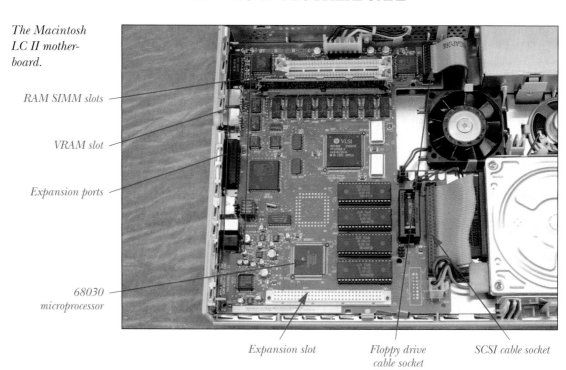

Expansion slot   *Floppy drive cable socket*   *SCSI cable socket*

MACINTOSH CENTRIS 650 MOTHERBOARD

The Macintosh Centris 650 motherboard.

VRAM SIMM slots

RAM SIMM slots

68040 microprocessor

Expansion ports

NuBus expansion slots

PDS (Processor Direct Slot) connector

MACINTOSH QUADRA 840AV MOTHERBOARD

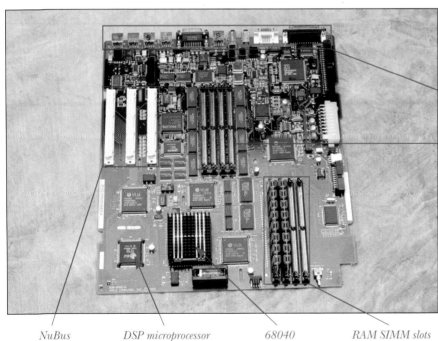

The Macintosh Quadra 840AV motherboard.

Expansion ports

VRAM SIMM slots

NuBus expansion slots

DSP microprocessor

68040 microprocessor

RAM SIMM slots

CHAPTER

4

Accelerator Cards

An Overview of Accelerator Cards

More speed is perhaps the most often heard desire of computer users. It seems that no matter how quick your computer is, you always want a bit more performance. With the constant parade of new Mac models, you are continually tempted by better, faster computers. Pretty soon, the Mac you have on your desk looks long in the tooth and could use a little pep. One way to get more computing punch is to add an accelerator card. These cards replace your computer's microprocessor with a faster model.

All Macintoshes introduced before the Power Macintosh line use microprocessors built by Motorola. The first Macs used the Motorola 68000 microprocessor. A few years later, the Macintosh II introduced the 68020 chip, which was about three times as fast as the 68000. Progress marched on, and the Macintosh IIx was the first Mac to use the 68030 processor, which is still used in some of the low-end Macs. The introduction of the Quadra line, with the Quadra 700 and 900, brought the 68040 processor. To get an idea of how Macs have improved, a Quadra 840AV, the fastest 68040-based Mac, is ten times faster than a Macintosh SE, running on a 68000. The high speed of the 68040 even requires a *heat sink*, a metal attachment that works to radiate the heat generated by the chip. The generic term for this family of microprocessors is the 680X0 family, with the X standing for any member of the processor line.

Speed of a particular microprocessor is given by its *clock speed*, measured in megahertz (MHz). A given clock speed of one type of microprocessor is not equivalent to the same clock speed of another kind of processor. For example, a 68040 chip running at 33 MHz gives far better performance than a 33 MHz 68030.

An important task of any microprocessor is to crunch numbers, and the 680X0 family has companion math chips that are designed for very fast mathematical calculations. These math chips are called *floating point units* (FPUs). The 68020's FPU chip is called the 68881; the 68030's FPU is the 68882; and the 68040 chip has a built-in FPU. A cheaper version of the 68040 without the FPU, called the 68LC040, is incorporated in several Mac models, including the Centris 610, the Quadra 605, and the PowerBook 500 series.

Floating point units are important primarily to three groups of Macintosh users. The first group is heavy spreadsheet users. The second group is high-end graphics mavens, especially those who use 3-D modeling and rendering programs. And the last group is scientific and engineering users, who typically use math-intensive programs. If you don't fall into one of these groups—for example, if you work mainly with word processing and database programs—chances are the presence of an FPU won't make much difference in the way you go about your work.

Most accelerator cards plug into the *processor direct slot* (PDS) on the Mac's motherboard. Accelerator cards are quick to install and reliable in operation.

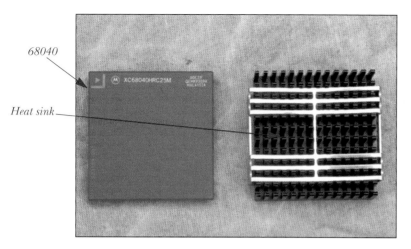

68040

Heat sink

A Motorola 68040 microprocessor with its heat sink removed.

A Motorola 68030 microprocessor.

CHOOSING AN ACCELERATOR CARD

Previously, when looking for acceleration, you had a choice between two approaches: an accelerator card or a motherboard upgrade. The latter, which is performed by an Apple dealer and exchanges your Mac's motherboard for a newer Mac model's motherboard, has been almost entirely discontinued by Apple. As of the summer of 1994, the only 680X0 motherboard upgrade still available for 68030-based machines was from the LC II or LC III to the 68040-based LC 475, which is the equivalent in the LC line to the Quadra 605. The only other motherboard upgrades are from Quadra or Centris Macs to Power Macs, which we cover in Chapter 5, "Upgrading to a Power Macintosh."

Many types of PDS accelerator cards are available, virtually for every Macintosh ever made. As a rule of thumb, it's best to invest in an accelerator card when the card can provide you with at least double the speed of your existing Mac. Be wary when you get smaller speed boosts. For example, a Mac SE can get a three or four times speed increase from a 25 MHz 68030 accelerator card, which sells for as little as $200. That's a good deal if you don't need color and want to squeeze another year or so of life from your SE. On the other hand, if you already have a 25 MHz 68040 Centris 650, a 40 MHz 68040 accelerator card will add a little zip, but it won't change your life. It will bite your wallet pretty hard, however, as it costs about $1,000. In this case, a Power Macintosh upgrade is probably a better choice.

APPROPRIATE ACCELERATORS FOR SOME MAC MODELS.

Macintosh Model	Type of Accelerator
68000-based Macs (Mac SE, Classic)	25, 33, or 50 MHz 68030
68020-based Macs (Mac II, LC)	33 or 50 MHz 68030
68030-based Macs (Mac SE/30, LC II, LC III, IIsi, IIci, IIvx, and others)	33 or 50 MHz 68030 33 or 40 MHz 68040
68040-based Macs (Centris/Quadra 610 and 650, Quadra 700 and 900)	40 MHz 68040

WHAT YOU'LL NEED

Minimal tools are necessary to install accelerator cards. You'll need the following items:

- The accelerator card.

- The software (if any) that came with the card.

- Whatever tools are needed to open the Mac's case (usually a Phillips or flat-blade screwdriver; see Chapter 3).

INSTALLING AN ACCELERATOR CARD

A DayStar Universal PowerCache with an adapter for a Mac IIsi.

IIsi adapter card   PDS connectors   DayStar PowerCache   68030 microprocessor   68882 FPU socket

We've illustrated a fairly common accelerator card, a DayStar Digital Universal PowerCache, installed into a Macintosh IIsi. The Universal PowerCache is a 50 MHz 68030 accelerator card with a socket for an optional 68882 FPU. You need an adapter in order to connect the DayStar accelerator to the IIsi's PDS slot. In other Macs, such as the IIci, IIvx, Performa 600, or any Centris or Quadra, no adapter is necessary. Follow these steps to install an accelerator card:

1 Shut down your Macintosh. Leave the computer plugged in to maintain a ground.

2 Remove the cover of your computer. Refer to the instructions in Chapter 3, "Getting Inside the Mac." If you have a computer that isn't mentioned in Chapter 3, refer to your Macintosh's manual.

3 Touch the metal portion of the power supply's case to discharge any static electricity that might be on your body or clothing, and then unplug the computer. (Refer to Chapter 3 if necessary.)

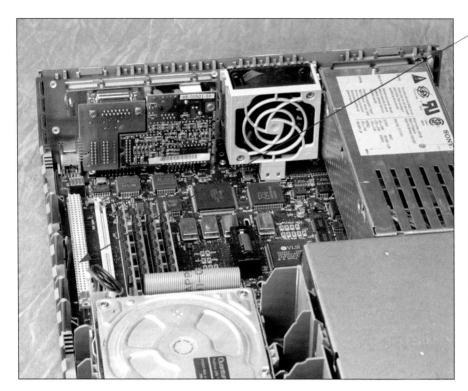

The Mac IIsi's PDS slot

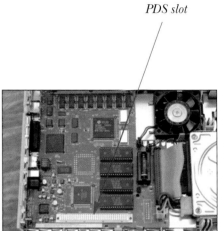

The Mac LCII's PDS slot

4 Find the processor direct slot (PDS) in your computer.

Connecting the accelerator card to the adapter card.

The assembled accelerator and adapter cards.

5 Remove the accelerator card and adapter (if any) from their protective packaging. Handle the cards only by their edges, and don't touch the PDS connector on the cards. Plug the accelerator into the female PDS socket on the adapter card.

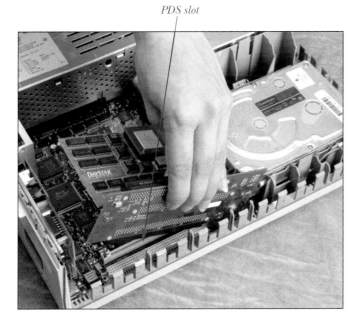

PDS slot

Inserting the accelerator/adapter combination into the PDS slot.

The accelerator/adapter cards fully installed.

In the Mac IIci, the DayStar accelerator plugs directly into the Mac's PDS slot without an adapter card.

6 Insert the adapter card's PDS connector into the IIsi's PDS slot, and press the top of the adapter card firmly until the connector is properly seated. There's no need to force the card. If you encounter resistance, remove the card and try again.

7 Replace the cover on your computer. (Refer to the instructions in Chapter 3 if necessary.)

8 Make sure all cable connections are secure, and then plug in your computer.

9 Turn on the Macintosh,

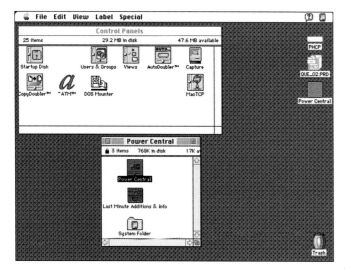

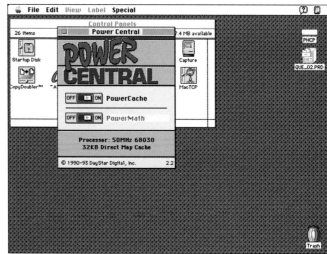

Drag the accelerator control panel to the Control Panels folder.

The accelerator control panel lets you switch the card on or off.

10 Install any software that came with your accelerator. This software is usually just a control panel that you need to drag to the Control Panels folder inside your System Folder. (That's for System 7 users. If you're running System 6.0.X, just drag the accelerator control panel to your System Folder.) After you have done so, restart your Macintosh.

11 If necessary, open the accelerator control panel and turn the accelerator card on.

TEST YOUR ACCELERATOR CARD

Your Macintosh should work normally, with the exception that you'll notice that all operations are faster. Windows open more quickly, programs load faster, and wait times for computations decrease. If the computer doesn't work correctly, check the following:

- Check to see if the accelerator's control panel (if one came with your card) was installed. Open the control panel and verify that the card is turned on.

- Did your Mac crash on startup? If so, you may have an incompatible extension or control panel. Power down the Macintosh, and then try starting up with the Shift key pressed (this prevents any extensions from loading). If the Mac boots normally, you almost certainly have an extension conflict, and you have to root out the culprit through trial and error. Pull all non-Apple extensions and control panels from their respective folders in the System Folder. Add them back in one at a time, rebooting after each addition, until your Mac refuses to boot. Next, remove the last item you added back into your System Folder. Contact the company that made the incompatible software to see if they have an upgraded version of the software.

- If you still can't get the Mac to boot, try doing a clean reinstall of the System software. For instructions, see Chapter 2, "Before You Get Started."

Upgrading to a Power Macintosh

POWER MAC UPGRADE OPTIONS

In March 1994, Apple introduced the Power Macintoshes, the first Macs to be based on a RISC microprocessor chip, called the PowerPC. RISC stands for Reduced Instruction Set Computing, and RISC processors are faster than standard processors such as the Motorola 68040 used in the Quadras, or the Intel Pentium processor used in many PC compatibles. The Power Macs are the first of a new breed; Apple has stated that it plans to move the entire Macintosh line to PowerPC over the next few years.

The Power Macs use a microprocessor called the PowerPC 601 that was developed jointly by IBM, Motorola, and Apple. The 601 is capable of blazing speed, up to three to ten times faster than a Quadra 840AV, the fastest 68040-based Mac. But to get this speed, programs must be rewritten to take advantage of the new processor. Apple, not wanting to make instantly obsolete the entire existing base of Mac software, created a 68040 *emulator*, built into the System Software, that allows the Power Macs to run software written for the 680X0 processors at about the speed of a Quadra 700. Compatibility of the emulator with existing 680X0 software is excellent; Apple claims that more than 98 percent of current Mac software runs without problems on the Power Macs, including applications, control panels, and system extensions. One drawback of the emulator, however, is that it doesn't emulate the FPU (floating point unit) in the 68040 processor. Programs that use a lot of floating point math and call the FPU directly, such as 3-D modeling and rendering software, don't work on the Power Macs. Luckily, most manufacturers of this kind of software have already released updates of their software in native PowerPC code and, as a result, are seeing speed increases of five to ten times over the 68040 version of the same software.

There are three basic models of Power Macintosh at this writing. They're called the 6100/60, 7100/66, and 8100/80, and they are based on the chassis of the Quadra 610, 650, and 800, respectively. The numbers after the slash represent processor speed; current PowerPC 601 chips come in versions that run at 60 MHz, 66 MHz, or 80 MHz.

As good as the performance is of the existing Power Macs, even better performance is still to come. By the end of 1994, a 100 MHz version of the 601 should be available, and Apple and IBM have shown a demonstration of a Power Mac with a 120 MHz 601 processor. The 601 is the first in a line of PowerPC microprocessors that will be released in the next two years. The PowerPC 603 is a low-power-consumption chip that is expected to have about the same performance as the 601 and is destined for future PowerBooks and small desktop systems. The 604 will have significantly better performance than the 601, and we should see Macs incorporating the 604 in mid to late 1995. Finally, the 620 chip, which should appear in late 1995, is a super-high-performance processor that is designed for network servers and high-end workstations.

For owners of older machines who want to upgrade to Power Mac performance, several upgrade options from Apple and DayStar Digital are available.

MOTHERBOARD SWAPS

The best, although most expensive, way to upgrade to a Power Macintosh is via a motherboard upgrade. With this upgrade, your dealer removes the motherboard (also called the logic board) of your existing computer and replaces it with a Power Macintosh motherboard. Actually, there's more than just the motherboard swapped when you buy a Power Macintosh Upgrade Kit. In fact, only the power supply, hard drive, CD-ROM drive (if any), and floppy drive from your old Mac are retained; they are transferred into a new case and chassis. In a very real sense, it's just as though you get a completely new machine.

A real deterrent to upgrading via a motherboard swap is cost. Let's say that you already have a Quadra 610. The upgrade kit to a 6100 has a list price of $999. It's very difficult to find significant discounts on motherboard upgrades, so the list price will be close to what you pay. As of the summer of 1994, the Quadra 610 was worth about $1,200 on the used market. Investing $999 into a $1,200 machine gives you a Power Mac 6100 that costs you $2,199. But you can buy a brand-new 6100 with 8 Mb of RAM and a 160 Mb hard drive for only $1,700. It would make more sense just to sell the Quadra 610 and kick in $500 to get a new 6100. You'll save $500. Even if you have a Centris 610, which is worth about $875 used, it's not a good deal. Upgrading to the 7100 or 8100 with Apple's motherboard upgrades give you similar financial results. It's almost always better to sell your existing Mac and buy a new one.

MACS UPGRADABLE VIA MOTHERBOARD SWAPS.

Motherboard Upgrade Kit	Eligible Macs
Power Macintosh 6100/60	Centris 610
Power Macintosh 6100/60AV	Quadra 610 Centris 660AV Quadra 660AV
Power Macintosh 7100/66	Macintosh IIvx, IIvi
Power Macintosh 7100/66AV	Performa 600 Centris 650 Quadra 650
Power Macintosh 8100/80	Quadra 800
Power Macintosh 8100/80AV	Quadra 840AV

POWER MAC UPGRADE CARDS

Apple offers a low-cost card ($699 list), the Power Macintosh Upgrade Card, that can upgrade some Quadra-level Macs to Power Mac capability without a motherboard replacement. The card plugs into the PDS slot on the Centris or Quadra 610, Centris or Quadra 650, and the Quadra 700, 800, 900, or 950. The Quadra 660AV and 840AV can't be upgraded with the Power Macintosh Upgrade Card because they don't have a PDS slot. The Power Macintosh Upgrade Card has a PowerPC 601 microprocessor on board, as well as the same 4 Mb Power Mac ROM chips found in all other Power Macs. The Apple card's operating speed depends on the base Macintosh in which it is installed. Because it uses a technique called "clock doubling," the Power Macintosh Upgrade Card runs its PowerPC 601 processor at twice the speed of the 68040's speed in the base Macintosh. The next table gives a complete breakdown of the Power Macintosh Upgrade Card's speed in various Macs.

POWER MACINTOSH UPGRADE CARD SPEED IN VARIOUS MACS.

Macintosh Model	68040 Speed (MHz)	Macintosh Upgrade Card Speed (MHz)
Centris 610	20	40
Centris 650	25	50
Quadra 610	25	50
Quadra 650	33	66
Quadra 700	25	50
Quadra 800	33	66
Quadra 900	25	50
Quadra 950	33	66

The Power Macintosh Upgrade Card has no RAM of its own. It uses the RAM on the motherboard of the host Mac, which must have a minimum of 8 Mb RAM. This lack of RAM on the upgrade card creates a performance bottleneck between the upgrade card, which is running with a 64-bit wide data path, and the motherboard RAM, which has a 32-bit data path to RAM. Apple has attempted to alleviate this slowdown by placing a huge 1 Mb of high-speed Level 2 cache RAM on the upgrade card. This cache acts as a buffer between the microprocessor and the motherboard RAM, smoothing performance. Even with this assist, when using native Power Macintosh software, the performance of a Mac with the upgrade card will usually be below that of a Power Macintosh 6100/60.

A benefit of the Power Macintosh Upgrade Card is that unlike a motherboard upgrade, you can turn it off and run with your Mac's standard 68040 processor if you have software that is incompatible with the Power Mac's excellent emulation, or if you need every bit of speed from older 680X0 software.

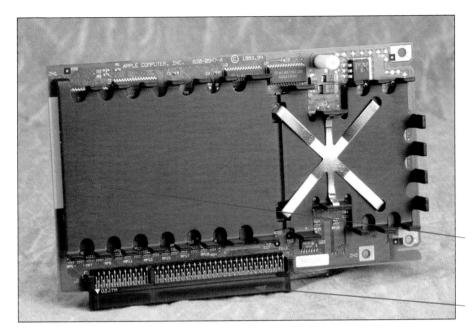

Apple's Power Macintosh Upgrade Card.

Heat sink

PDS connector

The Power Macintosh Upgrade Card with the heat sink removed to show some components. Do not remove the heat sink or you risk damaging the card! You should always install and run this card with the heat sink installed.

Power PC 601 microprocessor

High-speed cache RAM

An alternative to Apple's upgrade card is made by DayStar Digital, long known for accelerator cards using the Motorola 68030 and 68040. DayStar's upgrade card is called the PowerPro 601, and it plugs into a Quadra's PDS slot. It comes in two clock speeds, 66 MHz or 80 MHz. Unlike the Apple card, the PowerPro is clocked independently of the Mac in which it is installed; you get full-speed performance no matter which Mac the card is in. When the appropriate chips become available (in late 1994 or early 1995), the PowerPro will be upgradable to a PowerPC 601 processor running at 100

MHz. Because the card is independently clocked, it is faster than Apple's upgrade card. It is also more expensive. The suggested retail price of the 80 MHz version is $2,399 and the 66 MHz is $1,799. Included with the card is a set of Photoshop extensions manufactured by DayStar and Adobe. DayStar claims that in some Photoshop operations, the PowerPro 601 with these extensions is twice as fast as a Power Macintosh system. DayStar also includes other graphics software, including its PhotoMatic software, which automates many Photoshop functions.

The PowerPro 601 has a set of Power Mac ROM chips, licensed from Apple, and is fully compatible with all other Power Macs. It can be installed in the Centris or Quadra 650, and the Quadra 700, 800, 900, or 950. Because the PowerPro is a full-size upgrade card, it cannot fit inside the Quadra 610.

The PowerPro 601 has four slots that can take up to 128 Mb of RAM, using 60 ns 72-pin SIMMs. RAM on the upgrade card works faster than mother-board RAM, because of the board RAM's 64-bit data path to the processor. Because the PowerPro 601 can use the motherboard RAM in addition to its own, it allows you to stuff more RAM into your existing machine; up to 384 Mb on a Quadra 950. Graphics mavens who have loaded their Quadra 700, 900, or 950 machines with RAM, using the older 30-pin SIMMs, can use the PowerPro 601 to boost performance while still protecting their investment in that memory. If they went with a motherboard replacement, these users would have to get all new RAM, at significant expense.

Because of the relatively high prices of the PowerPro 601, it appeals mostly to high-end graphics users who want to make their existing Macs as fast as possible while maintaining absolute compatibility with 680X0 software.

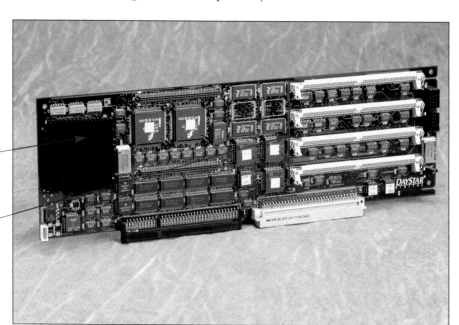

The DayStar Digital PowerPro 601 upgrade card.

PowerPC 601 microprocessor

Onboard RAM SIMM slots

MACS UPGRADABLE VIA PDS CARDS.

PDS Card	Eligible Macs
Apple Power Macintosh Upgrade Card	Centris 610
	Quadra 610
	Centris 650
	Quadra 650
	Quadra 700
	Quadra 800
	Quadra 900
	Quadra 950
DayStar PowerPro 601	Centris 650
	Quadra 650
	Quadra 700
	Quadra 800
	Quadra 900
	Quadra 950

WHAT YOU'LL NEED

Tools aren't usually necessary to install Power Mac upgrade cards. You need the following items:

- A compatible Macintosh with at least 8 Mb of RAM.

- The Power Macintosh Upgrade Card.

- The System Software that came with the card.

- A Phillips screwdriver (if installing in a Centris 610 or Quadra 610).

INSTALLING THE APPLE POWER MACINTOSH UPGRADE CARD

1 Shut down your Macintosh. Leave the computer plugged in to maintain a ground.

2 Remove the cover of your computer. Refer to the instructions in Chapter 3, "Getting Inside the Mac." If you have a computer that isn't mentioned in Chapter 3, refer to your Macintosh's manual.

3 Touch the metal portion of the power supply's case to discharge any static electricity that might be on your body or clothing, and then unplug the computer. (See Chapter 3 if necessary.)

PDS slot

PDS slot

Locating the Centris 650 PDS.

Locating the Quadra 700 PDS.

4 Find the processor direct slot (PDS) on your computer. There may be a NuBus card already installed in line with the PDS; if so, remove the NuBus card and reinstall it in another NuBus slot.

5 Take the Power Macintosh Upgrade Card out of its static-proof bag. Handle the card only by its edges, and don't touch the PDS connector on the card.

Note: The Centris 610 and the Quadra 610 require the use of a PDS slot adapter that is supplied with the Power Macintosh Upgrade Card. If you have one of these computers, refer to the manual packaged with the card for installation instructions.

Power Mac card plugs in here.

Attach metal shield here first.

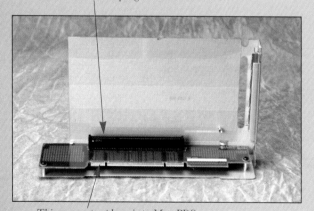

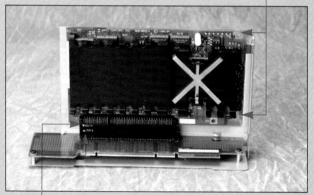

This connector plugs into Mac PDS.

Align these two arrows to correctly orient cord in adapter.

PDS slot adapter.

Power Macintosh Upgrade Card in the adapter.

Screw the metal shield onto the Power Mac card. Then orient the Power Mac correctly by aligning the arrow on the card with the one on the adapter. Screw the card onto the adapter. Remove the PDS port cover from the Mac case.

Positioning the upgrade card over the PDS slot.

The Power Mac Upgrade Card correctly installed in the Quadra 650.

6 Align the card's PDS connector with the PDS slot in your computer.

7 Remember to handle the card by its edges only, and don't press on the card's heat sink. Insert the PDS connector into the PDS slot and press the top of the card firmly until the connector is properly seated. There's no need to force the card. If you encounter resistance, remove the card and try again.

8 Replace the cover on your computer. Refer to the instructions in Chapter 3 if necessary. On the 610, use the thumbscrews to secure the cord and adapter to the case.

9 Make sure all cable connections are secure, and then plug in your computer.

10 Turn on the Macintosh.

11 Install the System software that came with your Power Macintosh Upgrade Card. To do this, insert the Installer disk in your floppy drive, and open the disk. Double-click the Installer icon. Click the Easy Install button in the Installer screen. The Installer will scan your hard drive and install updated system software. Your Mac will restart at the end of the system software installation.

12 The Power Macintosh Upgrade Card needs to be turned on before you can use native-mode Power Mac programs. Go to the Apple menu and choose Control Panels. Find the Power Macintosh Card control panel.

The Power Macintosh Card control panel.

Turning on the Power Macintosh Upgrade Card from the control panel.

Power Macintosh Card

At startup, the Power Macintosh Upgrade Card is:

⦿ On
◯ Off

If you change your startup option, you must turn off the computer for the change to take effect.

13 Open the Power Macintosh Card control panel. Click the On button.

14 Close the Power Macintosh Card control panel window, and then close the Control Panels window.

15 Choose Shut Down from the Special menu. Don't choose Restart, as the Power Macintosh Upgrade Card can only be turned on or off after you choose the appropriate action in the Power Macintosh Card control panel. Now power down the Macintosh.

16 Wait a few seconds, and then turn on your Macintosh. You should hear the Power Macintosh startup sound, which is different from the usual Quadra startup sound.

TEST YOUR POWER MACINTOSH UPGRADE

Your Macintosh should work normally, with the exception that you can now take advantage of the improved performance of Power Macintosh-native programs. If the computer doesn't work correctly, check the following:

- Did you hear the Power Macintosh startup sound? If not, make sure that the Power Macintosh Upgrade Card is seated properly in the Macintosh PDS slot.

- Did your Mac crash on startup? If so, you may have an incompatible extension or control panel. Power down the Macintosh, and then try starting up with the Shift key pressed (this prevents any extensions from loading). If the Mac boots normally, you almost certainly have an extension conflict, and you have to root out the culprit through trial and error. Pull all non-Apple extensions and control panels out of their respective folders in the System Folder. Add them back in one at a time, rebooting after each addition, until your Mac refuses to boot. Then remove the last item you added back into your System Folder. Contact the company that made the incompatible software to see if they have an upgraded version of the software.

- If the card is installed correctly and the Mac still doesn't start up, make sure that you have at least 8 Mb of RAM installed in the computer.

- If you still can't get the Mac to boot, try doing a clean reinstall of the System Software. For instructions, see Chapter 2, "Before You Get Started."

Chapter

6

Memory

AN OVERVIEW OF MEMORY

When you make a list of possible upgrades for your computer, chances are that upgrading the amount of memory in your computer will be close to the top of the list. You need memory so that you can open more programs at the same time, or when you want to work on bigger files in just one program. More memory also comes in handy so that you can use system add-on software, known as system *extensions*. These extensions add any number of great new capabilities to your Mac, from e-mail to macros, to disk protection, to screen savers and much more. But extensions, which load when your Mac starts up, eat up a portion of your computer's memory and usually keep the use of that memory. If, like many people, you have a couple dozen extensions running (at the moment I'm running 26 that I just couldn't live without), you can easily use 2 or 3 megabytes of memory. Add to that the approximately 2 megabytes that System 7 consumes, and you can use 5 megabytes of your total system memory before you even open a single program!

So what is memory, anyway? Memory is what a computer uses to store information while it is being processed. In effect, memory is where data goes while the Mac is "thinking." Physically, memory is contained on chips within your computer. The kind of memory that you'll be upgrading is called RAM (*random-access memory*). Sometimes you'll see RAM listed as DRAM; the D stands for *dynamic*. It's just another name for the same thing. RAM size is measured in *megabytes*, abbreviated Mb. RAM speed is measured in *nanoseconds*, or millionths of a second, abbreviated ns. RAM speed, however, doesn't affect the speed of your Mac; if you get faster RAM (or more RAM) your machine won't get any faster. To speed up your machine, you'll need an accelerator card (see Chapters 4 and 5 for more detail on accelerators). It's important to know the difference between memory and storage. Memory is temporary; the data in memory vanish when the computer is turned off. Storage—a hard drive, for example—is more permanent; data in storage remains until you erase it.

You add RAM to your Macintosh in the form of a small circuit board, called a SIMM (Single Inline Memory Module). A SIMM has memory chips on one or both sides and a row of flat connectors along one of its long edges. The connectors match up with pins in the SIMM socket on the Mac's motherboard.

A set of four SIMM sockets on a Quadra motherboard. The two rear sockets are empty; the front two have SIMMs installed.

Two main types of SIMMs are used with different kinds of desktop Macs. The older type, used in most Macs from the Macintosh Plus to the Quadra 950, has 30 connector pins, and the newer 72-pin kind is used in all desktop Macintosh models introduced since early 1993. This type includes the LC III, all the Centris models, the Quadra 605, 610, 650, 660AV, 800, and 840AV, and all the Power Macintoshes.

A 30-pin SIMM.

A 72-pin SIMM, showing chips on both sides of the board.

A few other kinds of memory have been used in past desktop Macs. The IIci had a special configuration that used *parity RAM*, a type of RAM designed to be slightly more reliable. The Macintosh IIfx used special 64-pin SIMMs.

MACINTOSH SIMM TYPES AND AVAILABLE SIZES.

SIMM Type	Sizes
30-pin SIMM	256, 512 Kb, 1, 2, 4, 8, 16 Mb
64-pin SIMM (Mac IIfx, some LaserWriters only)	1, 4, 16 Mb
72-pin SIMM	1, 4, 8, 16, 32 Mb

If you already have a 68030 or 68040 Mac with at least 4 Mb (preferably 8 Mb) of RAM, and you need to open more applications simultaneously, there's a stopgap measure that you can take before you have to buy more memory. It's a software package called RAM Doubler, by Connectix. This software fools your Mac into thinking that it has double the RAM that is actually installed. So if you have 8 Mb, the RAM amount that shows up in About This Macintosh is 16 Mb. If you have 20 Mb of physical RAM, you get 40 Mb of usable RAM. The amazing thing about RAM Doubler is that it actually works, and works well. It compresses the contents of RAM and then tells the Mac operating system that the uncompressed portions are now free, available RAM. With RAM Doubler, you can usually open multiple applications just as though you had double the physical RAM. The penalty you pay is slightly slower performance; on the order of a 5 to 10 percent slowdown, which is usually too small to notice. RAM Doubler is not a good choice for people who need to devote a large amount of RAM to one application, such as Adobe Photoshop. Photoshop and other graphics programs want all the RAM they can get, and RAM Doubler doesn't provide much help. For people doing word processing and other general tasks, however, RAM Doubler is terrific.

Another alternative to putting more RAM in your Mac is to use *virtual memory (VM),* which is a scheme that fools your Mac into thinking that part of your hard disk is RAM. The good part about VM is that it's free; it's part of the System Software on Macs that use System 7. You must have a 68030, 68040, or PowerPC-based Mac to use VM. The downside to VM is that because a hard disk accesses data in milliseconds and a RAM chip accesses data in nanoseconds, VM is much slower than real RAM. You access virtual memory from the Memory control panel under System 7.

Turn virtual memory on in System 7's Memory control panel.

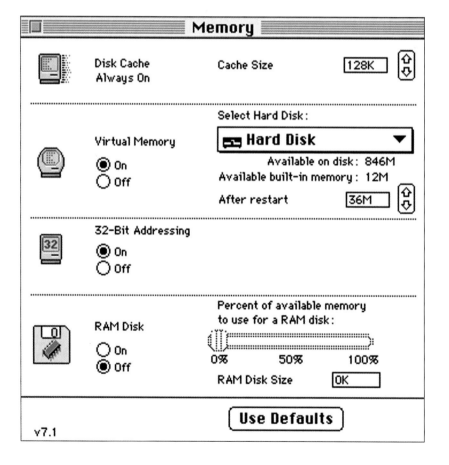

The best choice if you need more memory is to buy more RAM and install the SIMMs in your machine. The next best choice, and a cheaper alternative, is to use RAM Doubler. And finally, if you're really on a shoestring, use virtual memory.

Another option in the Memory control panel is *32-bit addressing*. This is a fancy way of saying "the ability to use more than 8 Mb of RAM." If you have more than 8 Mb of physical RAM in your machine, you must turn on 32-bit addressing. If you don't, your Mac will only be able to use 8 Mb of RAM, and it will show (in the About This Macintosh window in the Finder) amounts above 8 Mb as a larger amount of memory allocated to the System Software. This is a common problem with people who upgrade their RAM. Just click the On button in 32-bit addressing, and then restart the Mac to clear up the problem.

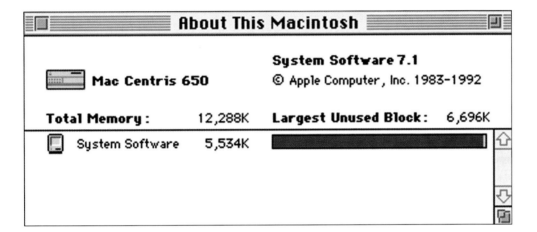

The About This Macintosh window on a Centris 650 with 12 Mb of RAM and 32-bit addressing off. Note the large size of the System Software.

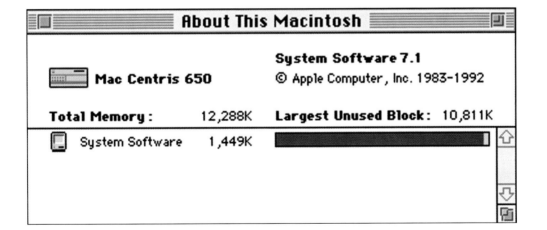

The same window, with 32-bit addressing turned on. Now the Mac can utilize all 12 Mb of RAM.

MEMORY REQUIREMENTS

How much memory do you need? Sometimes it seems like the answer is "as much as you can afford." Memory is like hard drive space; you could always use a bit more. The ballooning of applications and system software have raised the bar considerably in the past few years, and this trend shows no sign of abating. After System 7 was released a couple of years ago, the minimum RAM configuration became 4 megabytes. Eight megabytes of RAM is now the base configuration you should consider. If you have a Power Macintosh, plan on buying more RAM, because RISC programs require more RAM (and disk space) than their 680X0 counterparts.

In the real world of budgets and limitations, though, it's possible to figure out how much RAM you need depending on what kind of work you're doing with your computer.

If your Mac is mainly used for home use, games, personal finance, light word processing, and the like, you'll be able to get along just fine with 8 Mb of RAM.

If you use your Macintosh in a business setting, with heavy word processing, some light graphics, and presentation programs, and also have your Mac networked, then you'll want between 12 and 20 Mb of RAM.

If you work heavily with graphics programs like Adobe Photoshop and Illustrator, or page layout programs like Aldus PageMaker or Quark Xpress, 20 Mb of RAM just gets you started. You really do want all the RAM that you can afford, up to the limit of your Mac's capacity. People who work with desktop video are in the same boat. More, more, more!

RAM BY MODEL

The following table shows you how much RAM you can put into your machine, what kind of RAM to buy, and what sizes of SIMMs your Mac can accept.

MACINTOSH RAM CHART.

Macintosh Model	RAM SIMM Speed (ns)	RAM SIMM Type (# of pins)	RAM SIMM Sizes	Maximum
Centris 610	80	72	4, 8, 16, 32 Mb	68
Centris 650	80	72	4, 8, 16, 32 Mb	136
Classic	150	30	256 Kb, 1 Mb	4
Classic II	100	30	1, 2, 4 Mb	10
Color Classic	100	30	1, 2, 4 Mb	10
Color Classic II	80	72	1, 2, 4, 8 16, 32 Mb	36
IIci	80	30	256 Kb, 512 Kb, 1, 2, 4, 16, Mb	128
IIcx*	120	30	256 Kb, 1, 4, 16 Mb	128
IIfx	80	64	1, 4, 16 Mb	128
IIsi	100	30	256 Kb, 512 Kb, 1, 2, 4, 16 Mb	65
IIvi and IIvx	80	30	256 Kb, 1, 2, 4, 16 Mb	68
IIx	120	30	256 Kb, 1, 4, 16 Mb	128
LC and LC II	100	30	1, 2, 4 Mb	10
LC 475, 520, 550, 575, and LC III	80	72	1, 2, 4, 8, 16, 32 Mb	36
Macintosh II	120	30	256 Kb, 1, 4, 16 Mb	68
Macintosh TV	80	72	1, 2, 4 Mb	8
Performa 200, 400, 405, and 430	100	30	1, 2, 4 Mb	10
Performa 410	80	30	1, 2, 4 Mb	10
Performa 450, 460, 466, 467, 475, 476, 550, 560, 575, 577, and 578	80	72	1, 2, 4, 8 16, 32 Mb	36
Performa 600 and 600CD	80	30	256 Kb, 1, 2, 4, 16, Mb	68
Plus	150	30	256 Kb, 1 Mb	4

MACINTOSH RAM CHART. (CONTINUED)

Macintosh Model	RAM SIMM Speed (ns)	RAM SIMM Type (# of pins)	RAM SIMM Sizes	Maximum
Power Macintosh 6100/60 and 6100/60AV	80	72	4, 8, 16, 32 Mb	72
Power Macintosh 7100/66 and 7100/66AV	80	72	4, 8, 16, 32 Mb	136
Power Macintosh 8100/80 and 8100/80AV	80	72	4, 8, 16, 32 Mb	264
Quadra 605	80	72	1, 2, 4, 8, 16, 32 Mb	36
Quadra 610	80	72	4, 8, 16, 32 Mb	68
Quadra 650	80	72	4, 8, 16, 32 Mb	136
Quadra 660AV	70	72	4, 8, 16, 32 Mb	68
Quadra 700	80	30	1, 4, 16 Mb	68
Quadra 800	60	72	4, 8, 16, 32 Mb	136
Quadra 840AV	60	72	4, 8, 16, 32 Mb	128
Quadra 900 and 950	80	30	1, 4, 16 Mb	256
SE	150	30	256 Kb, 1 Mb	4
SE/30[*]	120	30	256 Kb, 1, 4, 16 Mb	128

[*] These machines require the 32-Bit System Enabler to access more than 8 Mb of RAM. This free extension from Apple allows the Mac to recognize additional memory.

WHERE IT GOES

The RAM SIMM slots are in a variety of locations on Macintosh motherboards. Although we can't show you the location of the SIMM slots on every motherboard, the following photographs show four representative Macs and the location of the RAM. If you have a model not shown, you should be able to locate the RAM by comparing it to one of the photos.

2 SIMM Slots

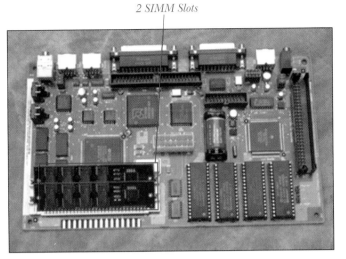

Mac Classic SIMM slots.

2 SIMM Slots

Mac LCII SIMM slots.

4 SIMM Slots

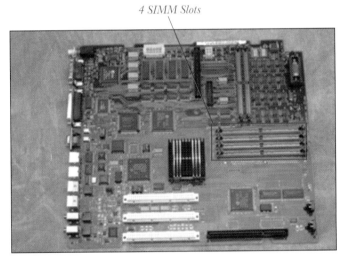

Centris 650 SIMM slots.

4 SIMM Slots

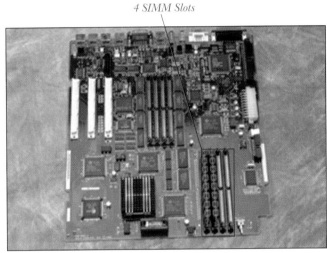

Quadra 840 AV SIMM slots.

WHAT YOU'LL NEED

You'll need the following tools to upgrade the RAM in your Macintosh:

- A Phillips screwdriver.
- A flat-blade screwdriver.
- The Mac Cracking kit (for compact Macs only; see Chapter 3).

REMOVING SIMMS

Here's how to remove SIMMs from any Mac motherboard. Follow these steps:

Releasing the SIMM slot's locking clips.

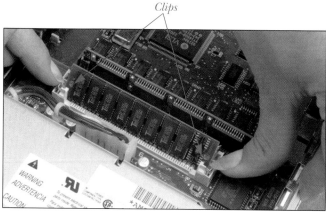

The SIMM has sprung backward now that the clips are released.

1 To remove a SIMM that is already in the SIMM slot, spread the metal locking clips at each end of the SIMM slot. The SIMM will probably spring forward a bit as the clips are released. Some SIMM sockets are set up in the opposite direction, so the SIMM might spring backwards.

> **Note:** On some older Macs, the clips on the SIMM sockets are made of plastic rather than metal. If this is the case on your Mac, take extreme care not to flex the clips more than they absolutely need to be in order to release the SIMM. You do not want to break the plastic clip; if you do, the SIMM may not seat properly and you may have to replace the motherboard.

Tilting the SIMM prior to removal.

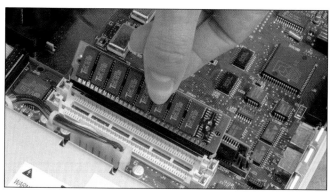

Lifting the SIMM out of its socket.

2 Tilt the SIMM forward (or backward, if you have that type of SIMM socket) and lift it out of its slot.

INSTALLING SIMMS

Here's how to install SIMMs onto any Mac motherboard. Follow these steps:

This alignment notch will match one on the slot.

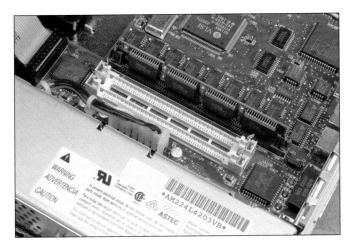

Two empty RAM SIMM sockets.

Positioning the SIMM over a SIMM socket.

1 Take the replacement SIMM out of its anti-static bag. Hold the SIMM by its top edge and insert it into the SIMM slot at a slight angle. Make sure that both ends of the SIMM's connector strip are evenly inserted in the slot.

Inserting the SIMM.

Locking the SIMM into place.

2 Applying even pressure across the SIMM, rock it backwards (or forwards, if you're working with that sort of SIMM socket) until it locks into place.

INSTALLING RAM IN SPECIFIC MAC MODELS

Although removing and installing SIMMs are basically the same operations in any Macintosh, you have to do very different things to get to the SIMM sockets in different Mac models. Here's a rundown of how to do RAM upgrades in four representative models. Refer to Chapter 3, if necessary, to see which of the following models is the most similar to your Macintosh.

UPGRADING RAM IN A CLASSIC II

To install RAM into a compact Macintosh, you need to remove the motherboard. Follow these steps:

1 Disconnect the Mac from the power supply, and remove the power cord from the back of the Mac.

2 Place the Mac facedown an a padded, grounded surface.

3 Remove the Mac's cover. Refer to the instructions in Chapter 3 if necessary.

Floppy drive   *Hard drive power cable*   *Cathode-ray tube (CRT)*   *Hard drive SCSI ribbon cable*

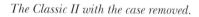

The Classic II with the case removed.

Removing the SCSI ribbon cable.

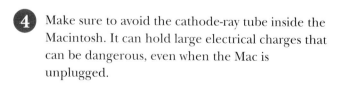

4 Make sure to avoid the cathode-ray tube inside the Macintosh. It can hold large electrical charges that can be dangerous, even when the Mac is unplugged.

5 Remove the SCSI ribbon cable from the motherboard. It's the wide flat cable at the rear of the motherboard.

Removing the floppy drive ribbon cable.

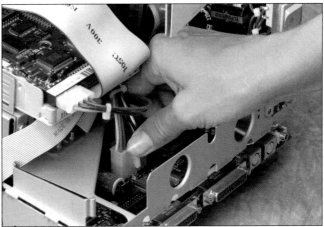

Removing the motherboard power cable.

6 Remove the floppy drive cable from the motherboard. It's the narrow flat cable at the rear of the motherboard.

7 Find the motherboard's power cable. It is a rectangular white connector in front of the SCSI cable's socket. Press down with your thumb on the cable's locking clip, grasp the connector by the white plug portion, and lift the plug out of the socket. Don't pull on the wires, and be careful that your hand doesn't bump into the back of the CRT when the cable comes loose.

8 For SE, SE/30 owners: Remove the small speaker cable. It's the small square orange connector near the power connector.

Removing the Classic II motherboard.

SIMMs installed in a Classic II.

9 Grasp the motherboard by its edges and slide it straight out of the chassis.

10 Find the SIMM sockets on the motherboard. Remove old SIMMs and install new ones according to the instructions in the previous sections.

11 Reverse the steps you took and reassemble the Macintosh.

Upgrading RAM in a LC II

Installing RAM in an LC-style machine is a fairly straightforward procedure. You don't have to disassemble the Mac; all you need to do is remove the top case.

1 Shut down your Macintosh. Leave the computer plugged in for now.

2 Remove the cover of your Macintosh. Refer to the instructions in Chapter 3 if necessary.

3 Touch your finger to the power supply to drain off any static electricity that might be on your body. Unplug the Macintosh.

4 Find the SIMM sockets on the motherboard. Remove old SIMMs and install new ones according to the instructions in the previous sections.

5 Put the cover back on.

Upgrading RAM in a Centris 650

To upgrade the RAM in a Centris/Quadra 650, you must remove the drive bays to get at the motherboard. Follow these steps:

1 Shut down your Macintosh. Leave the computer plugged in for now.

2 Remove the cover of your Macintosh. Refer to the instructions in Chapter 3 if necessary.

3 Touch your finger to the power supply to drain off any static electricity that might be on your body. Unplug the Macintosh.

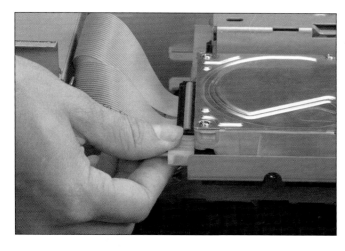

Removing the hard drive power cable.

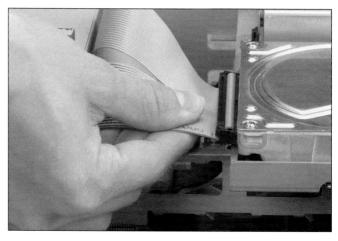

Removing the hard drive data cable.

4 Remove the hard drive power cable from the back of the hard drive.

5 Remove the hard drive SCSI cable from the back of the hard drive.

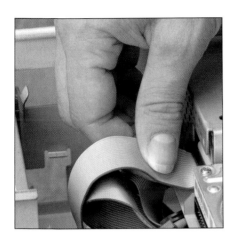

*Removing the
floppy drive cable.*

6 Remove the floppy drive cable from the back of the floppy drive.

7 If a CD-ROM drive is installed, remove its SCSI data cable, power cable, and audio cable.

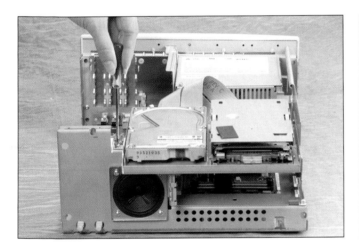

Removing the first chassis screw.

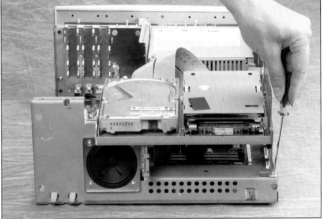

Removing the second chassis screw.

8 With the Phillips screwdriver, remove the two drive chassis screws.

*Removing the
power supply
screw.*

9 In the back of the Macintosh, remove the power supply screw from the rear bezel.

The power supply connectors are shown in detail in the next close-up.

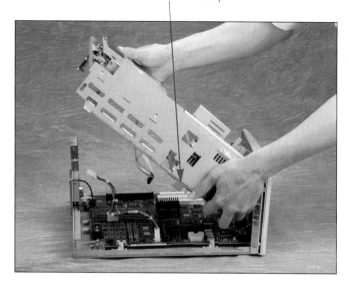

Lifting the drive chassis.

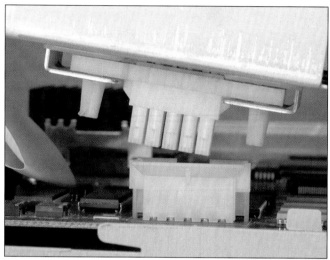

As you lift the chassis, the power supply will disconnect from the motherboard. This is a closeup of the power connector.

The Centris 650 with the drive chassis removed.

10 Lift the front of the drive chassis until it is perpendicular to the bottom case. Next, lift it forward and off the machine.

11 Find the SIMM sockets on the motherboard. Remove old SIMMs and install new ones according to the instructions in the previous sections.

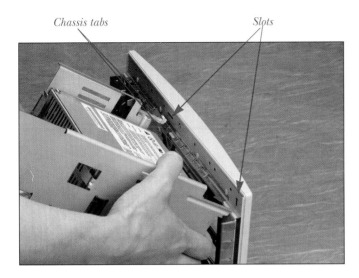

Positioning the drive chassis for reinstallation.

Reseating the drive chassis.

12 To reinstall the drive chassis, make sure that the metal tabs in the rear of the drive chassis fit into the slots in the bottom case.

13 Pivot the drive chassis down and into place. Make sure that the bottom corners of the drive chassis fit into the guides in the bottom of the case.

14 Reinstall the drive chassis screws and the power supply screw. Reinstall all internal cables. Replace the cover.

UPGRADING RAM IN A QUADRA 840AV

To upgrade RAM in a mini-tower Macintosh like the Quadra 800 or 840AV, you must remove the motherboard. Follow these steps:

1 Shut down your Macintosh. Leave the computer plugged in for now.

2 Remove the cover of your Macintosh. Refer to the instructions in Chapter 3 if necessary.

Side view of the Quadra 840AV with the case off.

— *Motherboard*

3 Touch your finger to the power supply to drain off any static electricity that might be on your body. Unplug the Macintosh.

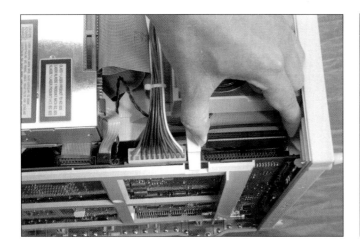

(Top view) Removing the SCSI data cable.

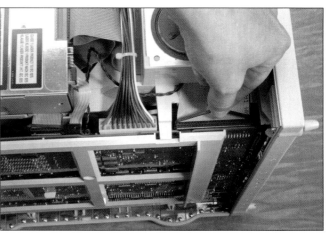

(Top view) Removing the power cable.

(Top view) Removing the speaker cable.

(Top view) Removing the CD-ROM audio cable.

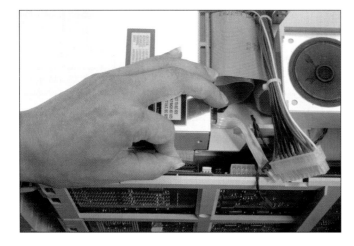

(Top view) Removing the floppy drive cable.

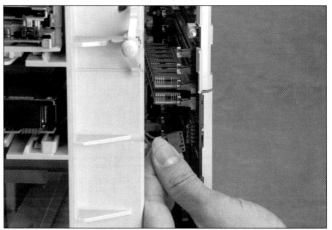

(Front view) Removing the LED cable.

4 Disconnect the following cables from the top of the motherboard:

SCSI data cable	CD-ROM audio cable (if present)
Power cable	Floppy drive cable
Speaker cable	LED cable

5 Remove the power-on actuator.

Removing the motherboard screw.

6 With the Phillips screwdriver, remove the screw that secures the motherboard.

Releasing the motherboard from the chassis.

Lift this latch.

Align these slots and tabs.

7 Slide the motherboard forward until the slot on the top edge of the motherboard lines up with the tab on the chassis. Lift the latch at the rear of the motherboard and release the motherboard.

Pivoting the motherboard.

8 Pivot the front of the motherboard away from the chassis.

Disconnecting the 840AV composite video cables.

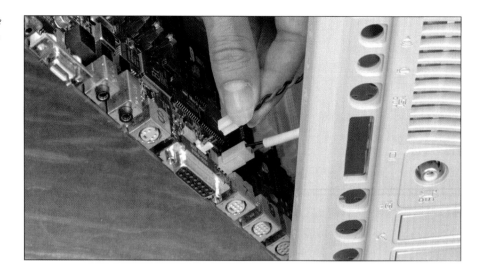

9 Disconnect the two composite video cables from their connectors at the rear of the motherboard (Quadra 840AV only).

10 Lay the motherboard flat on your work surface. Find the SIMM sockets on the motherboard. Remove old SIMMs and install new ones according to the instructions in the previous sections.

11 Take a break. You deserve it.

12 To put the Quadra 840AV back together, first stand the motherboard up next to the chassis. Reconnect the two composite video cables to their connectors at the rear of the motherboard. Guide the expansion ports in the rear of the motherboard into their corresponding holes in the rear case.

Pushing in the bottom of the motherboard.

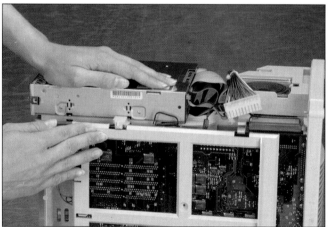

Pushing in the top of the motherboard.

13 Pivot the motherboard back towards the chassis. Press the bottom front of the motherboard into place.

14 Press the top front of the motherboard into place.

Reinstall the following:

>SCSI data cable
>
>Power cable
>
>Speaker cable
>
>CD-ROM audio cable (if present)
>
>Floppy drive cable
>
>LED cable
>
>Power-on actuator

 Reinstall the cover.

TROUBLESHOOTING

If your Mac doesn't work correctly after a RAM upgrade, you'll know right away. You'll attempt to start up your Mac and it won't work. Check the following:

- Right after you started the Mac, did you hear it make musical tones (not the usual startup sound)? If so, check to see whether the tones have one part or two parts. The tones are colloquially known as the Chimes O' Doom; they indicate that your Mac found something wrong when it performed its automatic hardware check on startup. If you heard one-part chimes, it's generally something wrong with the hard disk, floppy disk, or motherboard. If the chimes have two parts, however, that means that the Mac failed its RAM check on startup. Check to make sure that you seated all the SIMMs properly.

- Check that you're using the correct size and speed SIMM for your computer. You can tell how fast a memory chip is by looking at the numbers pasted on its top. After a long string of incomprehensible digits, you'll see a dash, followed by a number. That number, when multiplied by 10, gives you the rated speed of the RAM chips. So for example, a SIMM that has - 8 stamped on it means that the RAM on that SIMM is rated for 80 ns. Similarly, a chip with - 7 means that the chip is rated for 70 ns.

- Make sure that you are not using composite SIMMs on a Quadra 800, 840AV, or a Power Macintosh. Composite SIMMs are SIMMs that use physically larger chips in order to save money. Unfortunately, composite SIMMs make the above Macs act in a bizarre fashion and should be avoided.

- If you've added enough RAM to take your Mac above 8 Mb, make sure that you turn on 32-bit addressing in the Memory control panel, and then restart to take advantage of your new RAM.

Monitors, VRAM, and Video Cards

AN OVERVIEW OF MONITORS, VRAM, AND VIDEO CARDS

Upgrading your video system means one of two things: getting a larger monitor, or being able to display more colors on-screen. A larger monitor makes sense for many people, especially graphic artists who want to see more of their artwork at one time. With the proliferation of application programs that sport floating tool palettes, more screen real estate is bound to come in handy.

More colors are of use primarily to graphics users, too. Most Macs can display 256 colors (this color capacity is also known as "8-bit" color) on a 14-inch monitor using the built-in video. The next level is listed as "Thousands" in the Monitor control panel in your System Folder. It displays 32,768 colors and is also known as *16-bit* color. Finally, there's "Millions" in the control panel (16.7 million, to be exact), which is also known as *24-bit* color. The level of color that you're using is known as the *bit depth* or *color depth*.

The Macintosh Desktop and most games are optimized for 8-bit color. QuickTime movies are 16-bit. And high-quality photographs and photorealistic graphic files are 24-bit images.

The Macintosh built-in video is usually limited to 8-bit or 16-bit color, although a few Macs (the Quadra 700, 900, and 950, and the Power Macintosh 6100, 7100, and 8100) are capable of 24-bit color from the built-in video port. The color depth of a Mac's built-in video port is dependent on the amount of video RAM (VRAM) installed in the computer. The more VRAM, generally the more colors the Mac can display on a given size monitor, up to the limits of the hardware. For example, a Power Macintosh 7100 can display 16-bit color on a 17-inch monitor with standard 1 Mb of VRAM. Adding a 1 Mb VRAM SIMM allows the 7100 to display 24-bit color on the same monitor.

Video cards are most often installed to allow Macs that cannot display 24-bit color with the built-in video access to millions of colors. Video cards are also useful in that they free up the Mac's processor from the task of redrawing the screen, allowing for faster screen displays, especially when scrolling. Most video cards have special chips that accelerate QuickDraw (the ROM-based graphics routines built into every Mac).

A new wrinkle in monitors is the Apple AudioVision 14, a monitor designed for multimedia applications. The monitor has built-in stereo speakers, and a microphone for voice annotation or speech recognition.

MONITOR SIZES AND RESOLUTIONS.

Monitor Size (inches)	Resolution (pixels)
14-inch monitor	640 × 480
17-inch monitor	832 × 624
20-inch monitor	1024 × 768

MACINTOSH VRAM CHART.

Macintosh Model	Onboard VRAM	VRAM Slots	VRAM Speed	SIMM Size
Color Classic	256 Kb	1	100 ns	256 Kb
LC	0 Kb	1	100 ns	256 Kb or 512 Kb
LC II	0 Kb	1	100 ns	256 Kb or 512 Kb
LC III	512 Kb	1	100 ns	256 Kb
LC 475	0 Kb	2	80 ns	256 Kb or 512 Kb
LC 520	512 Kb	1	80 ns	256 Kb
IIvx	0 Kb	2	100 ns	256 Kb or 512 Kb
IIvi	0 Kb	2	100 ns	256 Kb or 512 Kb
Centris 610	512 Kb	2	80 ns	256 Kb
Centris 650	512 Kb	2	80 ns	256 Kb
Centris 660AV	1 Mb	0	80 ns	0
Quadra 605	0 Kb	2	80 ns	256 Kb or 512 Kb
Quadra 610	512 Kb	2	80 ns	256 Kb
Quadra 650	512 Kb	2	80 ns	256 Kb
Quadra 660AV	1 Mb	0	80 ns	0
Quadra 700	512 Kb	6	100 ns	256 Kb[**]
Quadra 800	512 Kb	2	80 ns	256 Kb
Quadra 840AV	1 Mb	4	80 ns	256 Kb
Quadra 900	1 Mb	4	80 ns	256 Kb[**]
Quadra 950	1 Mb	4	80 ns	256 Kb[**]
Power Macintosh 6100/60[*]	n/a	0	n/a	0
Power Macintosh 7100/66[*]	1 Mb	4	n/a	256 × 8 bit
Power Macintosh 8100/80[*]	2 Mb	4	n/a	512 × 4 bit
Performa 400, 405, 410, 430	0 Kb	1	100 ns	256 Kb or 512 Kb
Performa 450	512 Kb	1	100 ns	256 Kb
Performa 460, 466, 467	512 Kb	1	100 ns	256 Kb
Performa 475, 476	0 Kb	2	80 ns	256 Kb or 512 Kb
Performa 550	512 Kb	1	80 ns	256 Kb
Performa 600	0 Kb	2	100 ns	256 Kb or 512 Kb

[*] Power Macintosh models use DRAM based video and they are only expandable with the VRAM Expansion Card installed. The Power Macintosh 6100/60 is not expandable.

[**] VRAM SIMMs in the Quadra 700, Quadra 900, and Quadra 950 must be installed in pairs of two SIMMs.

The Apple Hi-Res 14-inch color monitor.

A SuperMac 20-inch Trinitron monitor.

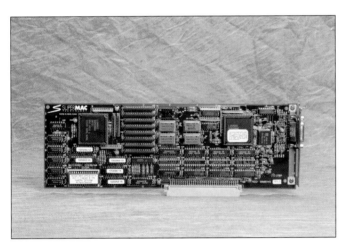

A SuperMac video card.

Microphone   *Speakers*

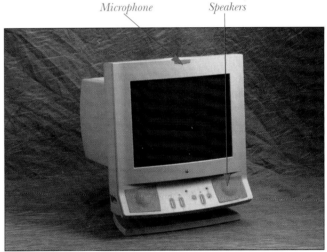

An Apple AV monitor.

WHAT YOU'LL NEED

If you'll be adding VRAM or a video card, you will need the same tools
required to open the Mac's case.

- A flat-blade or Phillips screwdriver.
- The new VRAM.

INSTALLING VRAM

Installing VRAM into your Mac is much like adding RAM memory. Follow
these steps:

1. Shut down your Macintosh. Leave the computer plugged in to maintain a ground.

2. Remove the cover of your computer. Refer to the instructions in Chapter 3 if necessary.

3. Touch the metal portion of the power supply's case to discharge any static electricity that might be on your body or clothing, and then unplug the computer.

VRAM SIMM

The VRAM slot inside the LC II.

Empty VRAM slots

VRAM SIMMs in the Centris 650.

VRAM SIMMs   *Empty VRAM slots*

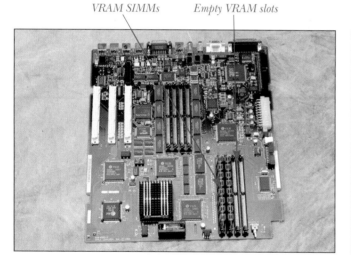

VRAM SIMMs in the Quadra 840AV.

Empty VRAM SIMM slots

The VRAM slots inside the Power Mac 7100/66.

4. Find the VRAM slot or slots in your computer. If the slot is empty, go to step 8. If a VRAM SIMM is already in the slot that you need, continue to the next step.

Clips

Releasing the SIMM slot's locking clips.

5 To remove a VRAM SIMM that is already in the VRAM slot, spread the metal locking clips at each end of the SIMM slot. The SIMM will probably spring forward a bit as the clips are released.

Removing the VRAM SIMM.

6 Tilt the SIMM forward and lift it out of its slot.

This alignment notch will match one on the slot.

Inserting the replacement VRAM SIMM.

7 Take the replacement VRAM SIMM out of its anti-static bag. Hold the SIMM by its top edge and insert it into the VRAM SIMM slot at a slight angle. Make sure that both ends of the SIMM's connector strip are evenly inserted in the slot.

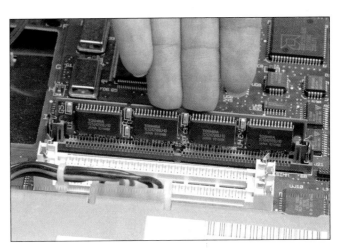

Snapping the VRAM SIMM into place.

8 Applying even pressure across the SIMM, rock it backwards until it locks into place.

INSTALLING A VIDEO CARD AND MONITOR

We've used a SuperMac video card and monitor for our example here. If you have another make of monitor, some steps may be slightly different. Follow these steps to install a NuBus video card in your Macintosh.

1 Shut down your Macintosh. Leave the computer plugged in to maintain a ground.

2 Remove the cover of your computer. Refer to the instructions in Chapter 3 if necessary.

3 Touch the metal portion of the power supply's case to discharge any static electricity that might be on your body or clothing, and then unplug the computer.

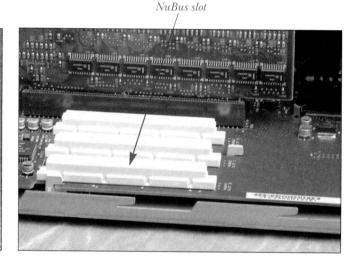

NuBus slot　　　　　　　　　　　*NuBus slot*

The NuBus slot on the Centris 650.　　　*The NuBus slot on the Power Mac 7100/66.*

4 Find the NuBus slots in your computer. Choose the slot in which you will install the video card.

*Pushing out the
NuBus cap.*

5 With your finger, push out the NuBus slot cap in the back of the case. Remove the cap.

6 Remove the video card from its antistatic bag. Remember to hold the card only by the edges, and don't touch the NuBus connector on the bottom of the card.

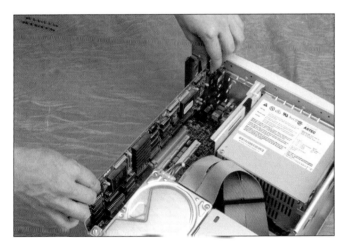

Positioning the NuBus card over the NuBus slot.

Seating the NuBus card.

7 Position the video card over the NuBus socket on the Mac's motherboard.

8 Gently press the card into place on the socket. If you have to use a lot of force, chances are you've mispositioned the card. Pull it out and try again.

9 Replace the cover of the Macintosh.

Monitor connector

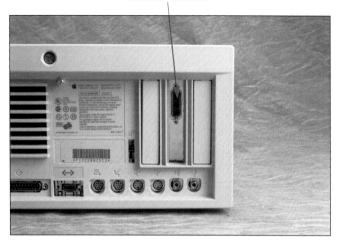

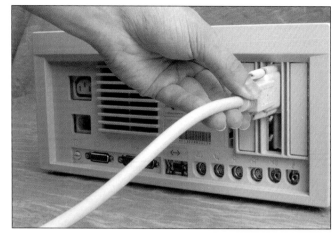

NuBus video card monitor connector.

Connecting the monitor cable.

10 The monitor connector will be visible from the back of the computer.

RGB video cable for a SuperMac monitor.

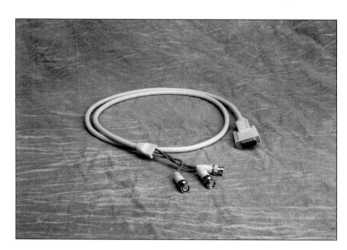

11 Unpack the monitor. Save the packing box, in case you ever have to send out the monitor for repair. You should have three pieces: the monitor, the video cable, and a power cable.

12 Plug the monitor cable into the socket on the video card. Make sure that it is evenly seated in the socket. Tighten the thumbscrews to secure the cable.

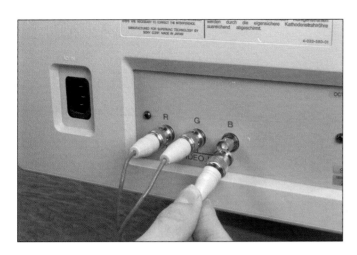

Connecting the RGB cable to the monitor.

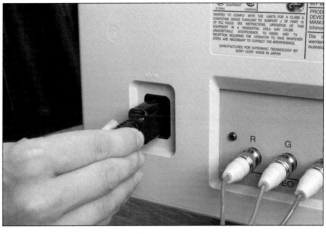

Connecting the monitor power cable.

 Connect the three video color cables to the BNC connectors on the back of the monitor. You need to press the connector onto the socket and then rotate the connector's cuff to secure the cable. Connect the red, green, and blue cables to the R, G, and B sockets, respectively.

 Plug the monitor's power cable into the back of the monitor, and then connect the other end to an electrical outlet.

TROUBLESHOOTING

If your monitor doesn't light up when you turn on your machine, check the following things:

- Check that the monitor is plugged in and turned on. Look for the little green power light on the front of the monitor.

- Make sure all your cables are secure.

- Check that the video card, if any, is seated properly.

- If you have video, but the picture has very distorted color, check that all the RGB cables are secure. With BNC connectors, they can often look as though they are on when they are actually loose. Take each one off; then reinsert it into the socket and secure it.

- If you get a really annoying high-pitched squeal from your monitor, it usually means that one of its internal components is about to fail. It may not fail immediately, however; it can remain working for months before it finally goes. If you can live with the squeal, do so. Otherwise you'll have to take the monitor to a shop for repair.

- You're upset because you've noticed a very thin (one pixel) black line that runs all the way across your Trinitron-based monitor, about three-quarters of the way down the screen. Don't be upset; it's perfectly normal. The black line is a shadow cast by a wire used inside the monitor tube to stiffen a component called a shadow mask. In fact, 16-inch or larger Trinitrons have two of these wires at about a third and two-thirds of the way down the screen. Don't worry about it. After a very short time, you won't even notice the black lines unless you look for them.

ADDING AN AV MONITOR

If your Macintosh supports the addition of an Apple AudioVision (AV) monitor, here are the steps to add it:

1 Turn off your Mac. Turn off the old monitor's power switch if it has one, and unplug its power cable.

2 Disconnect the video cable from the old monitor.

Connects to Mac Microphone plug *Connects to Mac speaker plug* *Connects to Mac ADB plug* *Connects to monitor cable*

Video cable for AV monitor.

Connects to Mac video port

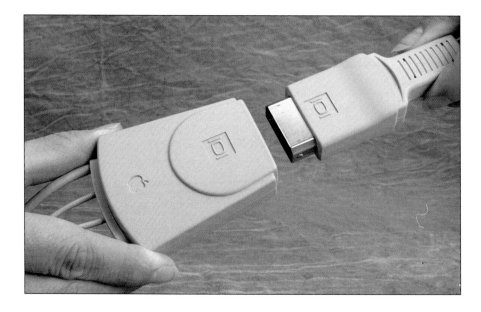

3 Unpack the monitor. Save the packing box, in case you ever have to send out the monitor for repair. You should have three pieces: the monitor, the video cable, and a power cable.

Connecting the two cables.

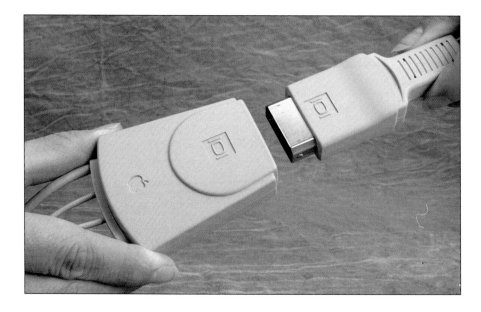

4 Connect the AV cable to the AV monitor cable.

Connecting the AV cables to the Mac.

—*Speaker*

—*Microphone*

—*Video connector*

—*ADB*

5 Connect the other ends of the cables to the appropriate plugs on the Mac. If you want to connect your keyboard and mouse to the monitor ABD ports, be sure to connect the ADB plug on the AV cable to the Mac.

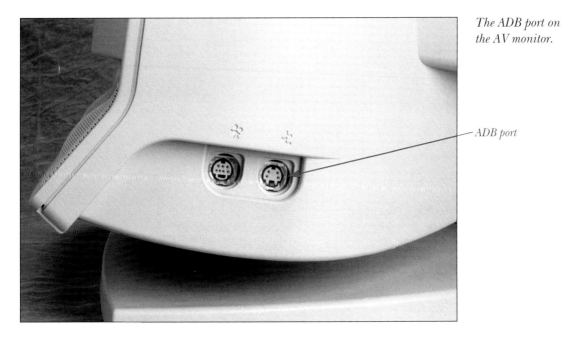

The ADB port on the AV monitor.

—*ADB port*

6 Connect the keyboard ADB cable to the monitor ADB port.

7 Plug the monitor's power cable into the back of the monitor, and then connect the other end to an electrical outlet.

8 Turn on the Mac.

Floppy Drives

AN OVERVIEW OF FLOPPY DRIVES

All Macintoshes, except the portable PowerBook Duo series, contain at least one 3.5-inch floppy disk drive—and usually one is all you need. Two floppy drives, as seen on discontinued Macs such as the Macintosh SE or the Macintosh II, were useful for two things: making floppy disk-to-disk copies and backing up the hard drive to floppies. With the capacities of current hard disks, it's no longer practical to use floppy disks as backup media. A 250 Mb hard disk, for example, would require almost 200 high-density floppy disks to back up. That would be an awful lot of disk swapping. As for making floppy disk copies, if you need only one copy, it's easy to swap two floppy disks a few times. If you need multiple copies of a floppy disk, Apple's Disk Copy program allows you to copy a whole floppy disk's contents into RAM and then copy it to as many disks as you need with one pass per disk. Other beneficial copy programs are the shareware DiskDup+ and the Floppier program in Symantec's Norton Utilities for the Macintosh.

The first three Macs released—the Macintosh 128K, the Macintosh 512K, and the Macintosh XL—had floppy drives that used single-sided disks that held only 400 Kb. Beginning with the Macintosh Plus in 1986, Apple switched to double-sided floppy drives with a capacity of 800 Kb. All Macs since the 1988 Macintosh IIx have a high-density floppy disk drive, called the SuperDrive, which can handle several floppy disk formats, including Apple's 800 Kb and 1.4 Mb, DOS 720 Kb and 1.44 Mb, the Apple II's ProDOS, and disks formatted under IBM's OS/2. By using Apple File Exchange or other translation software, you can easily read and write in any of these formats.

The only Macintoshes currently shipping that support external floppy drives are some PowerBook models. Discontinued models that supported an external floppy drive include the Macintosh Plus, SE, SE/30, Classic, Classic II, IIcx, IIci, IIsi, Portable, and Performa 200.

An external Apple floppy disk drive.

WHAT YOU'LL NEED

Tools aren't necessary to install an external floppy drive. You'll need the following items:

- Your Macintosh (it must be one of the models listed above, with an external floppy drive port).

- The external floppy disk drive.

INSTALLING AN EXTERNAL FLOPPY DISK DRIVE

To install an external floppy disk drive, follow these steps:

1 Shut down your Macintosh.

Floppy disk icon

The connector end of the floppy drive's cable.

The floppy drive port on the back of the Mac.

2 Look at the connector at the end of the cable that comes out of the external floppy disk drive. The floppy disk icon on the cable will match up with an identical icon on the back of your Mac.

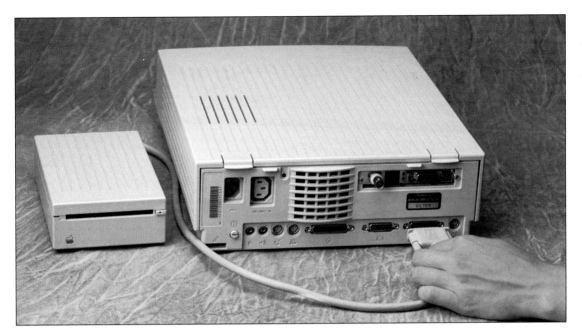

Attaching the floppy drive cable to the floppy drive port.

3 Plug the floppy drive's cable into the wide female floppy drive port on the Mac's back panel. Tighten the thumbscrews until they are snug, but don't overtighten them. The floppy drive is powered by the Mac; you don't have to worry about separate power connections.

4 Restart your Mac. The Mac should automatically recognize the new drive at startup.

TEST YOUR FLOPPY DISK DRIVE

Test your new acquisition by formatting a disk, and then by copying a few files from your hard disk to the floppy disk. If the Mac doesn't recognize the floppy drive, the problem will be one of the following:

- The floppy drive or the drive's cable is defective; try another drive.

- You didn't attach the floppy drive cable securely. Check the connector.

- It's unlikely, but the Mac's floppy drive port could be defective. If you try a second floppy drive and both drives don't work, you should take your Mac to a repair shop where they have diagnostic software to check out the floppy drive port.

CHAPTER

9

Hard Drives

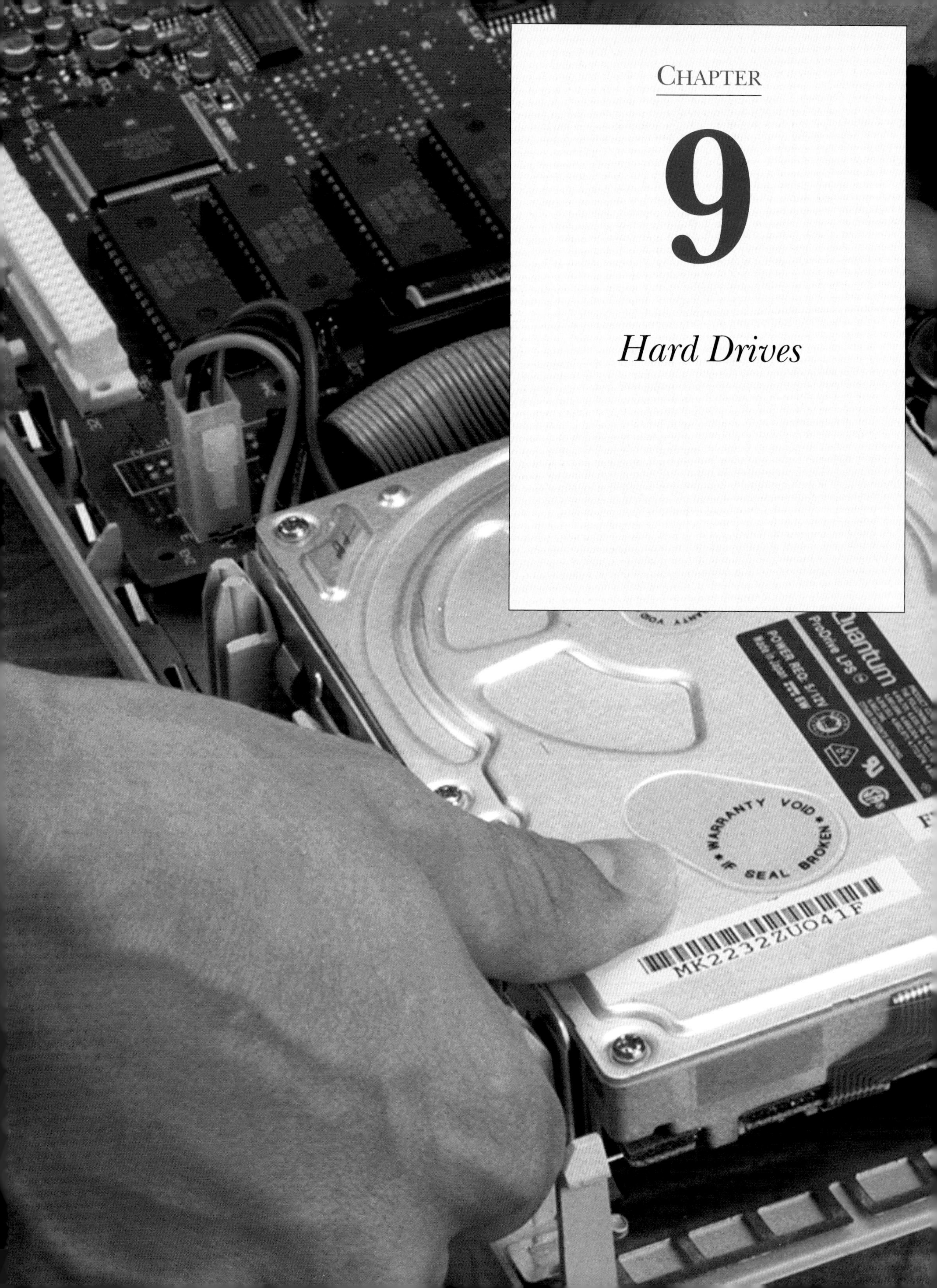

An Overview of Hard Drives

Other than more RAM, the most common upgrade for any computer is more storage space, and the best way to get more space is to buy a second hard drive, or to replace your current hard drive. The days where software manufacturers tried to keep their programs lean and mean are long gone; nowadays even word processors can take up more than 10 Mb on your hard disk. Programs like Adobe Photoshop make it easy to create graphic documents that are 50 Mb or more in size. After a dismayingly short time, it's not unusual to discover that your 80 Mb or 120 Mb hard drive is choked to capacity, and it's time to look for more storage. Owners of Power Macintoshes have it even worse; programs written for the PowerPC chip take up more disk space than those programs' 680X0 counterparts. In a surprisingly short time, all those people who bought their Power Macs with 250 Mb hard drives are likely to be looking for larger drives.

Before you go out and buy a new hard drive, consider a stopgap measure called *file compression*. These programs use software to rewrite the files on your hard disk in a form that is smaller; this is called *compression*. When you need the file, the software decompresses the file. This is usually done transparently; you won't even notice it happening most of the time. Several compression programs are on the market, and they all claim to approximately double the capacity of your hard drive. Most of them work well. Symantec's DiskDoubler, STAC's Stacker, and Aladdin's StuffIt SpaceSaver are the most popular. Compression programs like these are likely to stave off the time when you need to invest in a larger hard drive, but sooner or later that day will come.

Picking a Replacement Hard Drive

When you start to look for a new hard drive, the first question to ask is: "Where do you want the hard drive, inside your Mac or outside in an external case?" Putting a new drive inside will require you to remove the old drive and replace it with the new one (don't worry, it's not hard to do). You'll have to figure out what to do with the old internal drive; sell it, keep it as a spare, or put it into an external case for use with another Mac, or as extra storage for your current Mac (many drive vendors also sell empty external cases for old drives). If your new drive will be an external unit, you keep the old drive inside your Macintosh, maybe using it for just your System Folder and some applications, and you can move your documents onto the new drive. External drives are hooked up to your Macintosh via the SCSI port on the back of your Mac.

The next decision you need to make is how much storage capacity the new drive needs to have. Let's define some hard drive sizes. These days, drives from 80 Mb to 250 Mb fall into the category of small hard drive. The mid-range is occupied by 270 Mb to 540 Mb drives. And the large drives start at

1 gigabyte (abbreviated Gb, it stands for 1 billion bytes; a gigabyte is equal to 1,000 megabytes) and top out at a whopping 9 Gb. If you buy a *disk array,* where two drives are put together in the same case and the data is split between the drives, you can have up to 17 Gb of storage.

As a rule of thumb, don't bother buying a new drive that isn't at least twice the capacity of your current drive. Trust me, you're going to use that new space faster than you dream possible. People who are upgrading from a 40 Mb internal drive should set their standards even higher; it's easy to buy a internal 170 Mb drive for less than $200. A better choice is to buy the largest hard drive that your budget can afford. Squeeze a few extra dollars into the decision. You'll thank yourself later. Remember that it's easy to move a hard drive from one machine to another, so if you buy a big drive, you can use it when you upgrade to a new Mac.

A look at the ads in the Mac magazines will show literally dozens of hard drive vendors, most selling via mail order. Most of these vendors take hard drive mechanisms made by just a few manufacturers and package them into a case with formatting software. The largest drive mechanism manufacturers are Quantum, Seagate, Maxtor, Fujitsu, Micropolis, Conner, and IBM. All these manufacturers make good quality products that will serve your needs. Your choice is not so much the maker of the mechanism as the vendor of the completed drive. You also can buy drives from local computer dealers or from computer superstores.

What a drive vendor brings to a finished product is the quality of the case (for external units), warranty, technical support, and service. The hard drives market is cutthroat, driven by price more than anything else, but you will find that the best choice is not always the least expensive. Of the mail order vendors, it's a good idea to buy from the ones that have been around for a while. You may pay $20 more, but it will pay off with better support when you need it. APS, La Cie, and Club Mac all have good reputations. Of the vendors who sell mainly through storefront dealers, MicroNet, FWB, and PLI are good choices.

The quality most touted by many drive vendors is hard drive speed. Here's a secret: it hardly ever matters anymore. Hard drives have gotten so good that most of them will do just fine for most people's work. In real-world tests run by *Macworld* magazine, the difference between the fastest hard drive and the slowest in a given group of similar size drives is usually just a few seconds. Some users do need to worry about drive speed. Desktop video mavens, or people who do a lot of work in Photoshop (which has its own virtual memory scheme), or other folks who regularly work with files that are bigger than 10 Mb, should make the extra effort to look for a fast drive. But if you're doing mostly word processing or spreadsheets, don't worry about drive speed. It's especially a mistake to spend extra money to buy a super-fast drive and couple it with a Mac with a slower SCSI port. For example, a Macintosh IIci has a SCSI port with a maximum transfer rate of 1,800 kilobytes per second (kbps). Most hard drives in the 500 Mb range these days can transfer data at 2,000 kbps or more. So, in this case, the limiting factor in speed is the Mac, not the hard drive. By the way, if you have a Quadra, you shouldn't worry about its SCSI port being a bottleneck; most Quadras have SCSI ports that are rated at 3,800 kbps.

VOODOO, IDs, AND TERMINATION: SCSI EXPLAINED

The method that Macs use to connect to peripherals such as hard drives, CD-ROM drives, scanners, and some printers is called SCSI (pronounced "scuzzy"). SCSI (Small Computer Standard Interface) is an industry standard for hooking up to seven devices to your Macintosh. Devices are hooked up in a daisy chain, with connections from one device to the next. Each SCSI device on the chain must have a unique identifying number, called an *address*. SCSI addresses start at 0 and go up to 7. By convention, address 7 is always reserved for the Macintosh, and address 0 is reserved for the internal hard drive. This leaves six addresses for use by other devices. Every SCSI device has some method of setting the SCSI address. External devices have pushbutton switches or dials; internal devices' addresses are usually set by moving jumpers on the devices' controller board. It's very important that every device on the chain have a unique address; if two devices have the same address, usually one of them will not show up on the Desktop, or more likely, the computer will not boot at all.

At each end of the SCSI chain, you must have a device called a *SCSI terminator*. One end is no problem; the Mac's internal drive is already terminated. The device at the other end of the SCSI chain must either have a SCSI terminator that plugs into the back of the device, or must be internally terminated. Incorrect termination is usually the reason for problems with hooking up SCSI devices. For some reason scanners seem to be the most finicky kind of device.

Usually hooking up a few SCSI devices is not much of a problem. But on some occasions, you'll connect a new device and discover that it doesn't want to play by the normal SCSI rules. You'll terminate the last device, and the Mac still won't boot, or the device won't show up on your Desktop. This situation makes some folks consider SCSI termination a black art. But before you turn to animal sacrifice, consider a new solution, called *active termination*. This is where the drive, or a special powered SCSI terminator, senses the SCSI chain's requirements and provides the necessary termination. Several manufacturers build active termination into their drive cases, or you can buy external active terminators from APS or Relax Technologies. These terminators are highly recommended if you will be using more than just one or two SCSI devices.

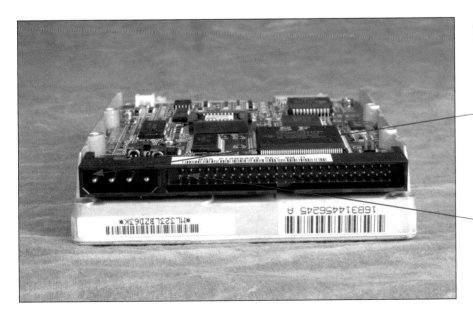

An internal hard drive mechanism

Power connector

SCSI ribbon cable connector

The terminating resistors on an internal hard drive.

Terminating resistor packs

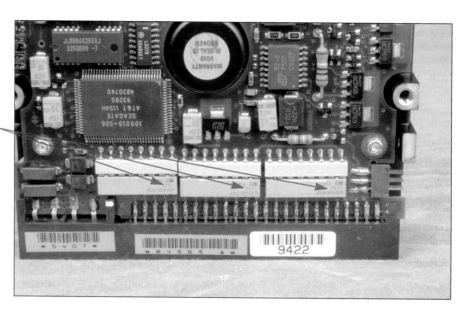

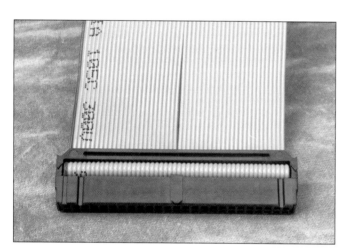

The business end of a SCSI ribbon cable.

Rectangular lug *Slot*

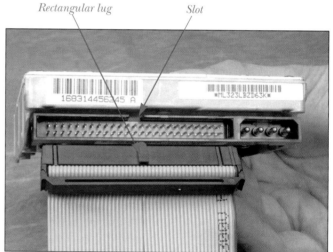

The SCSI ribbon cable, showing how it connects to a hard drive. Note the rectangular lug on the cable connector that fits into a corresponding slot on the socket.

REPLACING AN INTERNAL HARD DRIVE

The following instructions will serve for any Macintosh discussed in this book. We've used a Centris 650 to illustrate the steps but where the steps vary from model to model, we've shown our other example machines.

WHAT YOU'LL NEED

- The new hard drive mechanism.
- The Mac-cracking kit (for the all-in-one models).
- A Phillips screwdriver.
- A flat-blade screwdriver (for the Centris and Quadra models).

1 Disconnect the Mac from the power supply and remove the power cord from the back of the Mac.

2 Remove the Mac's cover. Refer to the instructions for your model in Chapter 3 if necessary.

Hard drive

The Classic II hard drive.

Hard drive

The LC II hard drive.

Hard drive

The Centris 650 hard drive.

Hard drive

The Quadra 840AV hard drive.

95

3 Locate the hard drive you are going to replace or the empty drive bay in your model.

Removing the power cable.

4 Remove the power cable from the back of the hard drive.

Removing the SCSI cable.

5 Remove the SCSI data cable from the back of the hard drive.

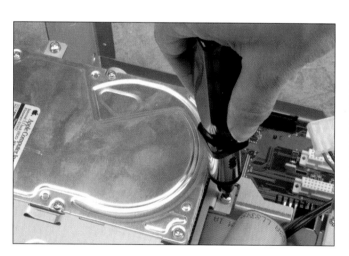

Unscrewing the drive from the Centris chassis.

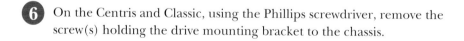
Unscrew these two screws.

These screws hold the hard drive carrier to the floppy drive housing in the Mac Classic.

6 On the Centris and Classic, using the Phillips screwdriver, remove the screw(s) holding the drive mounting bracket to the chassis.

Unsnap these clips.

On the Mac Classic, lift the hard drive out and remove the clip on the right side holding the wires in place.

On the LC II, spread the clips and lift the hard drive assembly out of the machine.

Retaining clip

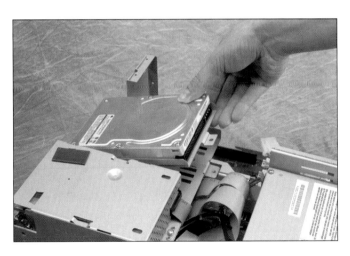

On the Centris, lift the old drive assembly up and off the chassis.

On the Quadra 840AV, press down on the plastic retaining clip at the front of the drive and slide the drive out.

7 Remove the old hard drive from the Macintosh and set it aside.

*Bracket mounting
screws*

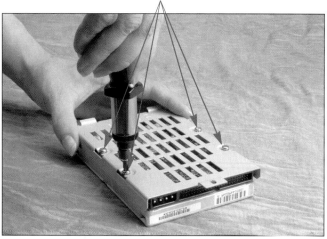

Removing the mounting bracket from the old drive.

Lifting the bracket off the old drive.

Positioning the bracket on the new drive.

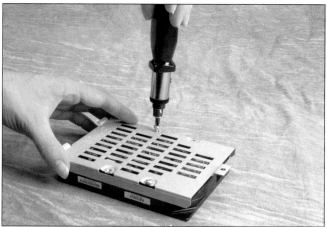

Attaching the bracket to the new drive.

8 For the Classic, the Centris, and the Quadra, if the new drive does not come with a mounting bracket, transfer the old drive's bracket to the new drive by first removing the four screws holding the bracket to the old drive, and then installing the bracket onto the new drive.

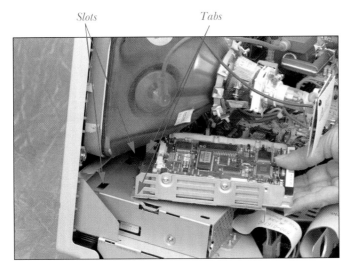

Slots   *Tabs*

Positioning the new drive in the Classic. Be sure that the tabs on the front of the hard drive carrier are inserted into the corresponding slots in the top of the floppy drive chassis.

In the LC II, position the new hard drive over the drive bay and gently press downward until it snaps into place.

In the Centris, make sure the tabs on the front of the bracket fit into the slots at the front of the drive bay.

In the Quadra, slide the new drive into the chassis about three-quarters of the way in.

 Place the hard drive into position on the chassis.

Screw in these two screws.

Replace these screws to hold the hard drive carrier to the floppy drive housing in the Mac Classic.

Securing the drive to the chassis in the Centris.

 10 On the Centris and Classic, screw in the Phillips screw(s) through the ear(s) on the drive mounting bracket.

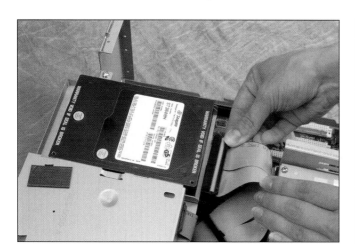

Connecting the SCSI cable.

Connecting the power cable.

 11 Plug the SCSI ribbon cable into the back of the hard drive.

 12 Reattach the drive's power cable.

 13 At this point, you can slide the drive the rest of the way in on the Quadra, until it snaps into place.

 14 Replace the Mac's cover and reattach all external cables. Plug in the Mac and start the machine. It should boot normally.

SCSI Termination Inside a 800-Style Quadra

SCSI termination inside the Quadra 800 or 840AV must be correct if the machine is to work. Inside these machines, only the last device on the internal SCSI chain is to be terminated.

Usually, the internal hard drive is the only device on the internal SCSI chain, and it is terminated by having its termination resistor packs installed. When installing a SCSI device in the 5.25-inch drive bay at the top of the Quadra, the internal SCSI ribbon cable is arranged so that device is the first in the chain. The next in the chain can be a device in the 3.5-inch third-height bay, and last would be a device in the bottom 3.5-inch half-height bay. The floppy drive is not a SCSI device; it needs no termination.

If a device is installed into the bottom bay, make sure that device is terminated and remove termination from all other internal SCSI devices.

As always, make sure that the SCSI address of each SCSI device is unique; no two devices, whether internal or external, can share the same address.

Installing an External Hard Drive

Installing an external hard drive involves the same procedure as hooking up any other external SCSI device. Keep in mind the usual SCSI address and termination issues.

What You'll Need

Tools aren't necessary to install an external hard drive. You'll need the following items:

- The external hard drive and its power cable.

- A 25-pin to 50-pin SCSI cable (if you're hooking the new drive directly to your Mac), or a 50-pin to 50-pin SCSI cable (if you'll be attaching the new drive to existing SCSI devices).

- A SCSI terminator if you don't already have one attached to an existing external SCSI device.

Installation: Step by Step

1   Shut down your Macintosh.

Two other types of SCSI ID selectors. To change the one on the top, insert a small tool in the hole and press to make it click. Change the one on the bottom by turning the dial with a small screwdriver.

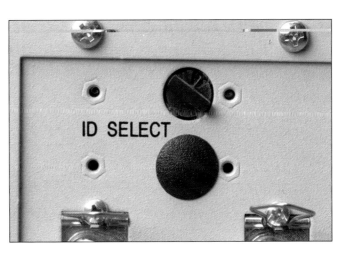

SCSI address switch.

2   Check the back of the hard drive for the SCSI address selector switch. This switch will be a pushbutton or rotary switch.

Changing the SCSI address.

3 If necessary, change the SCSI address of the drive so that it is different from any of your other SCSI devices.

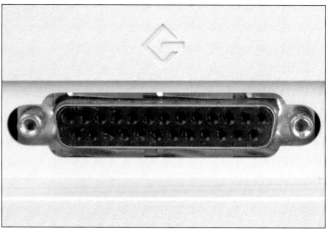

The Mac's SCSI port.

4 Find the SCSI port on the back of your Mac. It has an icon that looks like a diamond with a stick in it, or a really stylized letter "G."

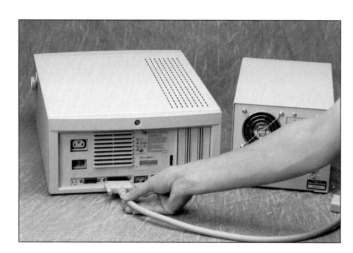

Connecting the SCSI cable to the Mac.

5 Connect the small end of the SCSI cable to the Mac's SCSI port. Turn the thumbscrews until the cable is snugly secured.

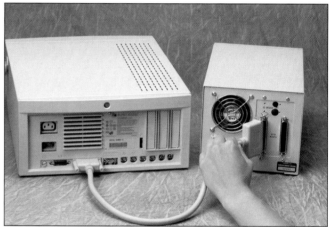

Hooking the SCSI cable to the hard drive.

6 Connect the larger end of the SCSI cable to the drive.

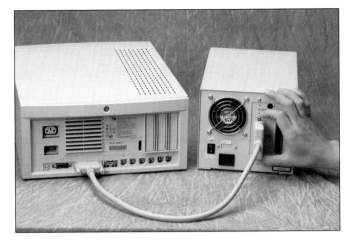

Snapping the wire holders into place.

Attaching the terminator.

7 Snap the wire holders on the hard drive's SCSI connector inside the ears of the cable's connector.

8 Attach a terminator to the other SCSI port on the drive and clip it into place.

9 Plug in the drive and turn it on. Then turn on the Mac. It should boot normally.

INSTALLING ADDITIONAL DEVICES ON THE EXTERNAL SCSI CHAIN

If you will be installing multiple external SCSI devices, this section will be helpful as it walks you through the steps for adding a second device. You add additional devices by repeating the same steps.

> **Note:** Adding a CD-ROM drive, tape drive, and other external SCSI devices are covered in detail in later chapters of this book.

1 Shut down your Macintosh, and turn off any external devices.

2 Check your other external device(s) to see what SCSI IDs are available and set an ID for the new device.

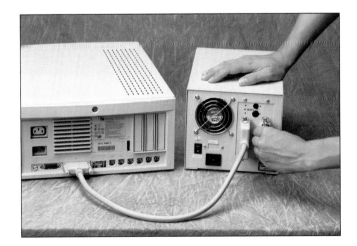

Removing the terminator.

3 Remove the SCSI terminator from the first device.

Attaching the SCSI cable.

 Attach one end of a 50-pin to 50-pin SCSI cable to the first device.

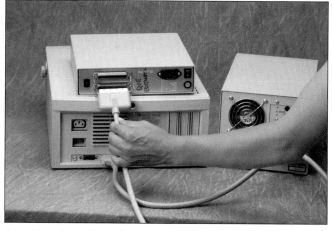

Attaching the cable to the second device.

 Attach the other end of the cable to the second external device.

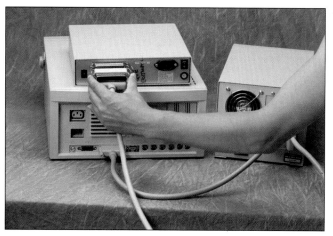

Attaching the terminator.

 Attach the terminator to the second (last) SCSI device.

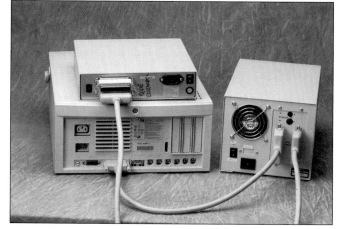

The completed SCSI chain.

 The SCSI chain is now complete. Plug in the external devices; then turn them on and start up your Mac.

TROUBLESHOOTING

If your Macintosh doesn't boot after you install a new hard drive, it's usually because you have two SCSI devices set to the same address. Other things to check include:

- Are the SCSI and power cables secure?

- Is the power switched on for all external devices?

- Check that the device at the end of the SCSI chain is terminated.

AN OVERVIEW OF CD-ROM DRIVES

A CD-ROM drive is a terrific addition to your computer system. CD-ROMs allow you to bring incredible amounts of information to your Desktop and to access that information quickly. CD-ROMs can contain reference books, vast amounts (up to 600 Mb) of computer software, multimedia games, compressed full-motion video that you can play on your computer screen, and much more.

CD-ROM stands for Compact Disc Read-Only Memory. As the name implies, you can read information from a CD-ROM, but you cannot write data to it, nor can data be erased. A cousin to the standard audio CD, a CD-ROM disc can contain music as well as data, and all Macintosh CD-ROM drives can play audio CDs. The benefit of CD-ROM is that it can hold so much data in an easily transportable and storable package. A drawback is that drive speed, and therefore data retrieval, is much slower than with a hard disk.

You can buy three speeds of CD-ROM drive—single, double, and triple speeds. Single-speed drives are obsolete; you shouldn't buy one. The most common type sold today is the double-speed variety; you can buy a good double-speed drive for as little as $299. Finally, a few triple-speed drives are available. These drives are faster but cost considerably more than a double-speed drive. Compare double- and triple-speed drives before you buy to make sure that the cost differential is worth it to you.

CD-ROM drives are all SCSI devices and require that you install driver software into your Mac's System Folder before your Mac will recognize a CD. Once that's done, a CD shows up on your Desktop just like any other disk volume, except that because you can't write to it, the CD-ROM will always show up as locked.

An external Apple CD300 CD-ROM drive.

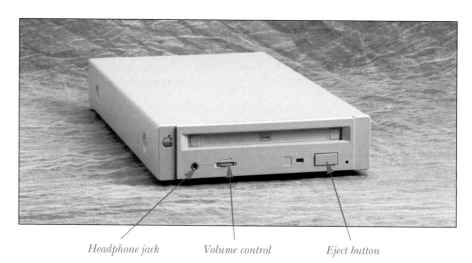

Headphone jack   *Volume control*   *Eject button*

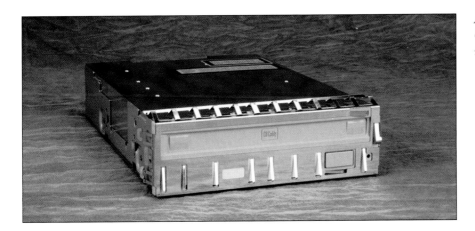

*An internal
CD-ROM drive
mechanism.*

INSTALLING AN INTERNAL CD-ROM DRIVE

CD-ROM drives can be installed into the 5.25-inch drive bay of the Centris/Quadra 610 and 660AV, the Centris/Quadra 650, the Macintosh IIvx, the Quadra 800, 840AV, 900, and 950, and the Power Macintoshes.

WHAT YOU'LL NEED

To install your internal CD-ROM drive, you need the following items:

- The CD-ROM drive mechanism.

- The plastic mounting bracket and screws that came with the CD-ROM drive (Quadra 800-style machines only).

- The metal mounting bracket and screws that came with the CD-ROM drive (Quadra 650 style machines only)

- The internal audio cable that came with the CD-ROM drive.

- A flat-blade screwdriver (to open the Mac's cover).

- A Phillips screwdriver.

INSTALLING AN INTERNAL CD-ROM DRIVE

To install your internal CD-ROM drive, follow these steps:

1 Shut down your Macintosh. Leave the computer plugged in for now.

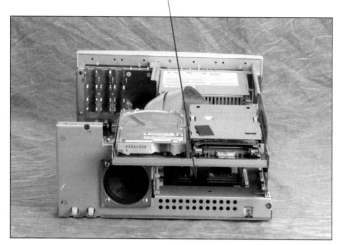

The CD-ROM drive will be installed here.

The Centris 650 with the case removed.

The CD-ROM drive will be installed here.

The Quadra 840AV with the case removed.

Note: If your CD-ROM has a SCSI that is set by three jumpers labeled 0, 1, 2 (see photo below), use this table to determine the SCSI ID.

SCSI ID	PINS JUMPERED		
	0	1	2
0*			
1	X		
2		X	
3	X	X	
4			X
5	X		X
6		X	X
7*			

*IDs 0 and 7 are not allowable for a CD-ROM.

2 Remove the cover of your Macintosh. Refer to the instructions in Chapter 3 if necessary.

3 Touch your finger to the power supply to drain off any static electricity that might be on your body. Unplug the Macintosh.

The rear panel of the CD-ROM mechanism.

Audio connector

SCSI data connector

Power connector

4 Take a look at the back of the CD-ROM drive and locate the three connectors you'll be using.

The SCSI ID on this internal drive is set by jumpers.

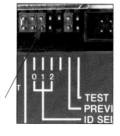

Jumpers

Note: The SCSI ID on an internal CD-ROM drive is usually set by the manufacturer. Check the documentation that came with your drive to determine the SCSI ID that the drive is set to, and then make sure that the ID is unique. It may be easier to change the ID of any external devices if there is a conflict.

Carrier   *Screws*

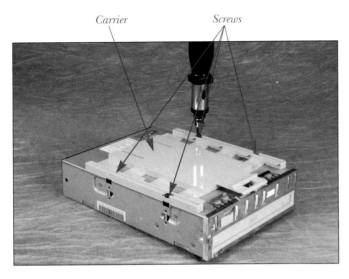

Attaching the carrier for the Quadra 840AV to the CD-ROM mechanism.

Sliding the CD-ROM drive into the drive bay.

5 When you bought the CD-ROM drive, it should have come with the drive rails or carrier already in place. If they are not in place, screw the rails onto the CD-ROM drive mechanism with four small Phillips-head screws.

6 Take the CD-ROM drive, and slide it into the 5.25-inch bay. On the Centris-like models, don't slide the drive all the way in. You'll need some room to attach cables.

Locking tab

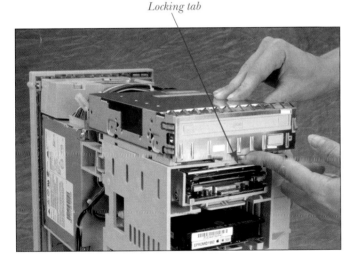

Securing the carrier.

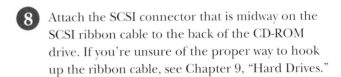

Connecting the SCSI data cable.

7 On the Quadra 840AV, you need to lift up on the tab at the front of the carrier as you slide the carrier back to snap the drive into place.

8 Attach the SCSI connector that is midway on the SCSI ribbon cable to the back of the CD-ROM drive. If you're unsure of the proper way to hook up the ribbon cable, see Chapter 9, "Hard Drives."

Note: With machines like the Quadra 650 and 800 that can accept multiple internal SCSI devices, there is still only one logical SCSI chain. In this case, of the seven possible SCSI devices, two or three will be internal, and the rest external. Usually, the internal 3.5-inch hard drive in the Macintosh is the only SCSI device on the internal SCSI chain. Therefore, that device would be terminated, as is the motherboard. When you install a SCSI device into the internal 5.25-inch drive bay, the internal SCSI cable is set up so that the 5.25-inch device is the first in the chain, and the 3.5-inch hard drive the last. It's important to make sure that the 5.25-inch device has its termination resistors removed. When you buy a new internal CD-ROM drive, these resistors should already be removed.

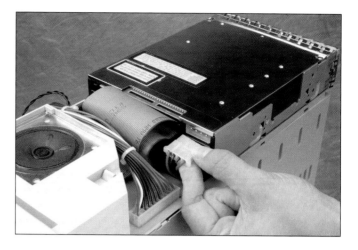

Connecting the power cable.

9 Plug the power connector into the back of the CD-ROM drive. The connector is keyed so that it can go in one way only.

Connecting the audio cable to the motherboard.

Connecting the audio cable to the CD-ROM drive.

10 Plug one end of the audio connector into the back of the CD-ROM drive. Connect the other end to the connector on the motherboard (it's an orange connector towards the back of the motherboard, near the NuBus slots).

11 At this point, on the Centris, you can now slide the CD-ROM drive back into the bay until it snaps into place.

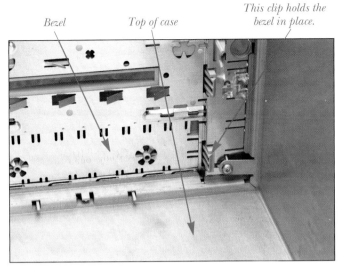

Bezel   *Top of case*   *This clip holds the bezel in place.*

Removing the original bezel.

Snapping the new bezel into place.

12 From the inside of the cover, remove the existing bezel by pressing in on the tabs and pushing the bezel out.

13 Install the slotted CD-ROM bezel provided with your drive.

14 Reinstall the cover of the Macintosh. Refer to Chapter 3 if you need instructions.

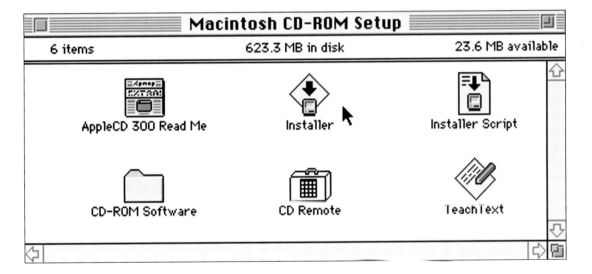

Starting the Installer.

15 Turn on the Mac, and install the driver software that came with your CD-ROM drive. To do this, insert the floppy disk that came with the CD-ROM drive. Double-click the disk icon to open it. Double-click the icon for the Installer program.

Installing your CD-ROM driver.

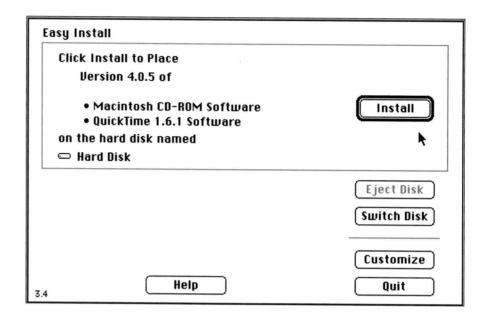

16 When the Installer screen appears, click the Install button. The Installer program will place on your hard disk the software your Mac needs to use the CD-ROM drive. When the Installer is done, it will present a dialog box informing you that the software installation is complete. Click the Quit button to leave the Installer.

17 Restart your Mac so that the computer can use the new software.

INSTALLING AN EXTERNAL CD-ROM DRIVE

Installing an external CD-ROM drive is much like installing any other SCSI device, with the addition of installing an audio cable and driver software.

WHAT YOU'LL NEED

Tools aren't necessary to install an external CD-ROM drive. You'll need the following items:

- The CD-ROM drive and power cord.

- One SCSI cable, either 25-pin to 50-pin (if you're hooking the drive directly to the Mac) or 50-pin to 50-pin (if you're connecting the drive to another SCSI peripheral).

- A SCSI terminator (if the drive is the last device on the SCSI chain).

- The driver software that came with your drive.

INSTALLING AN EXTERNAL CD-ROM DRIVE

To install your external CD-ROM drive, follow these steps:

1 Shut down your Macintosh.

The Mac's SCSI port.

Hooking the SCSI cable to the CD-ROM drive.

2 Find the SCSI port on the back of your Mac. It has an icon that looks like a diamond with a stick in it, or a really stylized letter "G."

3 Connect the small end of the SCSI cable to the Mac's SCSI port. Turn the thumbscrews until the cable is snugly secured.

4 Connect the larger end of the SCSI cable to the drive. Snap the wire holders on the CD-ROM drive's SCSI connector inside the ears of the cable's connector.

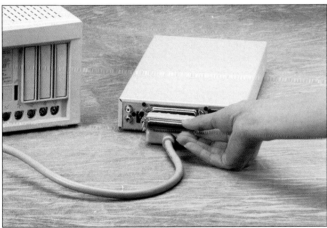

The SCSI cable and terminator on the CD-ROM drive.

Securing the SCSI terminator to the CD-ROM drive.

5 If the drive is the last SCSI device on the SCSI chain, you must attach a SCSI terminator to the other large connector on the back of the drive. If the removable drive is in the middle of the chain, the terminator should be on the last device.

6 Snap the wire holders on the CD-ROM drive's SCSI connector inside the ears of the SCSI terminator's connector.

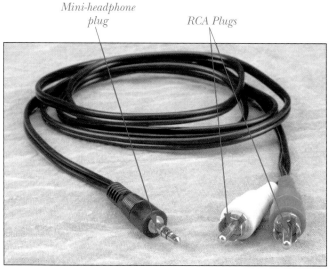

Mini-headphone plug   *RCA Plugs*

Changing the SCSI address.

The CD-ROM audio cable.

7 Check on the back of the drive for the SCSI address selector switch. This switch will be a pushbutton or rotary switch.

8 If necessary, change the SCSI address of the drive so that it is different from any of your other SCSI devices.

9 Find the audio cable. It has two RCA-style plugs on one end and a mini-headphone plug on the other.

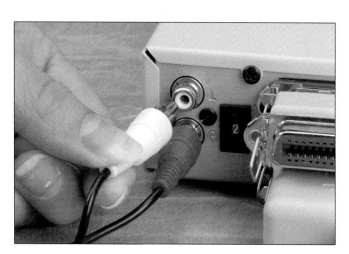

Attaching the audio cable to the CD-ROM drive.

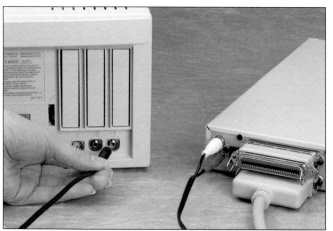

Attaching the audio cable to the Mac.

10 Plug the audio cable's RCA plugs into the audio jacks on the back of the CD-ROM drive. If the audio jacks are color coded, match them to the colors on the plugs. If not, the red plug should go in the right channel jack and the other plug should go in the left jack.

11 Plug the other end of the audio cable into the sound input port on the back of your Macintosh. It has an icon that looks like an old-style microphone.

12 Connect the power cable to the drive and plug it in.

13 Turn on the Mac, and install the driver software that came with your CD-ROM drive. To do this, insert the floppy disk that came with the CD-ROM drive. Double-click the disk icon to open it. Double-click the icon for the Installer program. (See the section on installing an internal CD-ROM drive to see the screens that display during software installation.)

14 When the Installer screen appears, click the Install button. The Installer program will place on your hard disk the software your Mac needs to use the CD-ROM drive. When the Installer is done, it will present a dialog box informing you that the software installation is complete. Click the Quit button to leave the Installer.

15 Restart your Mac so that the computer can use the new software.

TEST YOUR CD-ROM DRIVE

Test your new drive by inserting a CD-ROM disc in the drive. The CD-ROM should appear on your Desktop, just like any other disk. If you have problems, check the following:

- Was the driver software installed?

- Are all the cables securely connected?

- Is the CD-ROM drive turned on?

- Is there a CD-ROM disc in the drive?

- Is the CD in the drive properly (with the label side up)?

An Overview of Tape Drives

There are two kinds of computer users: people who *have* lost their data to a hard drive crash or other problem, and those who *will* lose their data. If you're in the first group, chances are you've learned from the experience and are now backing up your hard drives. If you're in the second group, you should know that having a recent backup can mean the difference between an inconvenience and a disaster.

Tape drives are one of the best methods of inexpensive, reliable backup. Tape is far superior to other backup media on a basis of cost per megabyte of storage. For example, an 88 Mb SyQuest cartridge sells for about $68, which works out to 77 cents per megabyte. The lowest capacity (60-meter) DAT tape holds 1.3 gigabytes (Gb) and costs about $13. That's only a penny per megabyte! 90- and 120-meter tapes give you even better bang for the buck. Because tapes are so cheap, it's easy and feasible to make more than one copy of your precious data and store the extra copy off-site so that all of your backups aren't destroyed in the case of a catastrophe that wipes out your office.

Removable drives, such as the SyQuest 88 Mb, have an apparent advantage over DAT in that the drive mechanism is considerably less expensive. From one mail order company, for example, a SyQuest 88 Mb drive costs $429, versus $799 for a DAT drive. But if you look at the total costs for a given amount of storage, tape wins out easily. Take the 1.3 Gb DAT drive, which comes with one tape cartridge. Total investment is $799. To get the same amount of storage from the 88 Mb SyQuest, you would have to buy 14 extra cartridges, for a total investment of $1,381. Suddenly, the lower up-front cost of the SyQuest drive isn't that important.

Types of Tape Drives

All tape drives for the Mac are SCSI devices, and most are external units. The Quarter-Inch-Cartridge (QIC) drives were the first tape backup units for the Macintosh. They use quarter-inch wide tape, called the DC2000 format, encased in a hard plastic cartridge shell with a machined aluminum base plate. While still very popular for IBM-compatible computers, DC2000 drives have a variety of drawbacks which have led to their decline in the Mac market. They are limited to low (120 Mb) capacity; they're noisy and slow; and they are almost twice as expensive to operate as any of the other drives on the market, with tapes costing about 25 cents per megabyte. The Apple Tape Backup 40SC, now discontinued, was a DC2000 drive that had a capacity of 38 Mb. A fair number of these drives are still in use, although their sluggish performance is outclassed by virtually all other tape drives now available. There are two formats used the most for backup on the Mac today: Teac and helical.

TEAC

There are three Teac data cassette drives, which hold 60 Mb, 150 Mb, and 600 Mb, respectively. Each mechanism uses a different kind of cassette, and the larger capacity models can read, but not write, the lower capacity formats. The 60 Mb drive has been discontinued, supplanted for personal backup by the faster 150 Mb drive.

A Teac 150 Mb drive is a fair entry point for people who have light backup needs. The drives are inexpensive; a Teac 150 Mb drive sells for as little as $450. Their capacity is a bit small for people with newer Macs that come with 250 Mb hard drives. If you still have older, smaller drives, however, the Teac 150 units are a decent backup choice. Tapes cost about $20, which breaks down to 13 cents per megabyte of storage. Several manufacturers offer Teac 150 Mb drives, and price and technical support should be your prime buying considerations.

The highest capacity version of the Teac mechanism holds 600 Mb. At street prices of under $700, the Teac 600 drive isn't really competitive with low-end DAT units, which you can buy for $750, and are faster and hold more than twice as much data. Although they are solid, reliable units, the Teac 600 drives are not recommended due to price.

DAT AND 8MM

If you want to back up a large amount of data, you need a drive that combines huge capacity and high speed. Helical drives fit the bill. They're called *helical* because the tape is wrapped around a drum with spinning read and write heads that trace a diagonal path across the tape. There are two main types of helical drives, 8mm and DAT. Both types are based on consumer-electronic tape formats; 8mm tape was originally designed for camcorders, and DAT mechanisms found their start in digital audio tape recorders. Both 8mm and DAT backup drives have been extensively modified from their origins, however. You won't be able to use your camcorder for backup. Data backup requires higher reliability than video or audio reproduction, so helical backup drives include, besides the SCSI interface that lets you hook it up to your Mac, error-correction circuitry and higher quality tape transports than their consumer brethren.

DAT tapes come in three lengths, 60, 90, and 120 meters. Without using data compression, 60 meter tapes hold 1.3 Gb of data, the 90 meter tapes have a capacity of 2 Gb, and the 120 meter tapes take 4 Gb. DAT drives that incorporate a chip that compresses the data as it is being written to the tape are able to fit more data on a given tape and are the fastest tape backups. Be careful of compression claims, however. Some manufacturers claim that compression allows them to squeeze as much as 8 Gb on a 90 meter tape. While this is theoretically possible, it is very unlikely in a real-world situation; most files cannot be compressed to such an extent. Applications tend not to compress well; sound and font files even less. Best for compression are text, word processing, and bitmapped graphic files. A more realistic figure for a 90 meter compressing DAT's capacity is between 3 and 4 Gbs, depending on the kinds of files being compressed.

An external DAT tape drive.

The top of the heap in tape capacity is held by the 8mm helical drives. All 8mm drive mechanisms are made by one manufacturer, Exabyte. There are two versions of the 8mm drive, holding 2 to 5 Gb and 5 to 10 Gb, respectively, the exact capacity depending on data compression. Because all the drive mechanisms are the same, your choice of an 8mm drive should be based on price, service, and which manufacturer's software makes the mechanism perform best. The 8mm drive format is the current leader in capacity, and it is expected to maintain that lead as technologies improve and capacities in all formats increase. Besides backup, 8mm drives are also popular with high-end desktop video users, who can use 8mm drives to transfer video animation between the Macs and other video and computer systems.

A DAT tape cartridge.

What You'll Need

Tools aren't necessary to install an external tape drive. Installing an internal tape drive in a Macintosh Quadra 650, 800, 840AV, 900, or 950, or a Power Mac 7100/66 or 8100/80, is very similar to installing an internal CD-ROM drive. Please refer to Chapter 10, "CD-ROM Drives," if you want to install an internal tape drive. You'll need the following items:

- The tape drive.

- A SCSI cable (if the drive is external).

- A SCSI terminator (if the drive is external and will be at the end of a SCSI chain; see Chapter 9, "Hard Drives," for more information).

- A Phillips or flat-blade screwdriver to open the Mac case (if the drive is internal).

Installing an External Tape Drive

You add an external tape drive in the same way that you add any external SCSI device. Follow these steps:

1 Shut down your Macintosh.

SCSI address switch.

2 Check on the back of the tape drive for the SCSI address selector switch. This will be a pushbutton or rotary switch.

Changing the SCSI address.

3 If necessary, change the SCSI address of the tape drive so that it is different from any of your other SCSI devices. (See Chapter 9 for details on SCSI addresses.)

The Mac's SCSI port.

4 Find the SCSI port on the back of your Mac. It has an icon that looks like a diamond with a stick in it, or a highly stylized letter "G."

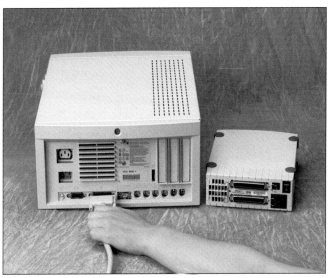

Connecting the SCSI cable to the Mac.

5 Connect the small end of the SCSI cable to the Mac's SCSI port. Turn the thumbscrews until the cable is snugly secured.

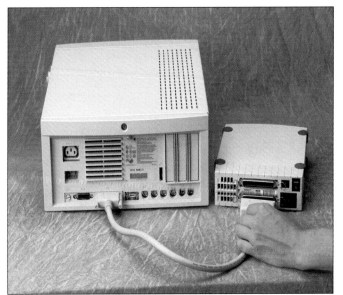

Hooking the SCSI cable to the tape drive.

6 Connect the larger end of the SCSI cable to the tape drive. Snap the wire holders on the tape drive's SCSI connector inside the ears of the cable's connector.

8 Plug the tape drive in, turn on the tape drive, and then turn on the Mac. Following the instructions that came with the unit, install the backup software that came with your tape drive.

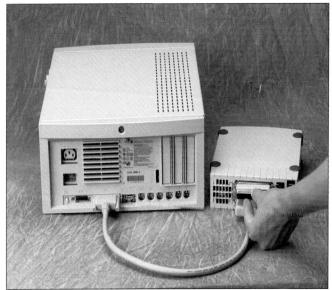

The SCSI cable and terminator on the tape drive.

7 If the tape drive is the last SCSI device on the SCSI chain, you must attach a SCSI terminator to the other large connector on the back of the tape drive. If the tape drive is in the middle of the chain, the terminator should be on the last device.

TEST YOUR TAPE DRIVE

Test your new tape drive by using it and the backup software to back up your internal hard drive. If the software can't find the tape drive, or if the lights on the front of the drive remain dark, check all the drive's cable connections.

Other things to check if you have problems include the following:

- Check the SCSI address of the tape drive, making sure that it is different from the addresses on all the other SCSI devices you have installed.

- If the Mac doesn't boot, check to make sure that the SCSI chain is properly terminated, as explained in Chapter 9.

An Overview of Removable-Cartridge Drives

A removable-cartridge drive is a SCSI storage device in which the data is stored on a disk inside a plastic cartridge that can be taken out of the drive mechanism. You should consider removable storage as an upgrade for your Mac system for a number of reasons. First, there's portability. It's easy to take a cartridge across town to another location when you need to transport a large amount of data. For example, you might take a SyQuest cartridge with your 30 Mb PageMaker file to your service bureau for printing on the bureau's Linotronic imagesetter. A second reason to go removable is to increase your storage capacity. If you're running out of space on your hard drive, removables offer almost unlimited expandability; you just add another cartridge when you need more storage. A third rationale for removable storage is for backup; a few cartridges can back up the data on most small to medium size hard drives, up to about 300 Mb. If you have more data than that to back up, you should look to a tape backup drive. Lastly, you can use removable cartridges for security. You can store your sensitive work on a cartridge and lock the cartridge up in your safe at the end of the workday.

Three main types of removable-cartridge drives are used with the Macintosh: SyQuest, Bernoulli, and magneto-optical. A brief rundown of each type follows.

SyQuest Drives

With the exception of floppy disks, these drives are the most popular type of removable storage for the Mac. They have hard plastic cartridges that contain a metal hard disk platter. The cartridge also has a hinged door that opens when the cartridge is inserted into the drive to give the drive's read/write heads access to the disk platter. These drives are reliable and fairly fast, although not as fast as a regular hard disk (none of the removable media drives are).

Among graphics users, SyQuest drives long ago became the standard for moving around large amounts of data. You can be fairly confident that any service bureau you patronize will have a 44 or 88 Mb SyQuest drive available for your cartridges.

SyQuest drives (and cartridges) come in two sizes and five capacities. The drives are most often used as external devices, though they can be installed internally in the 5.25-inch drive bay of the Macintosh IIvx, Centris/Quadra 650, and the Quadra 800 and 840AV.

SYQUEST CAPACITIES.

Drive Model No.	Capacity (Mb)	Media Size (inches)
SQ555	44	5.25
SQ5110c	88/44	5.25
SQ5200	200	5.25
SQ3105	105	3.5
SQ3270	270	3.5

All SyQuest mechanisms are built by SyQuest and are simply packaged by each manufacturer. Still, the kind of case the SyQuest mechanism goes into is important; a well-built case, with a decent cooling fan and high-quality power supply and cables, will perform better and longer than a cheaper case. You should pick a SyQuest drive based on the manufacturer's reputation for quality, technical support expertise, and price.

A SyQuest drive, with the cartridge in place.

This button and lever eject the cartridge.

This 5.25-inch SyQuest cartridge holds 44 Mb of data.

Hard disk platter (inside cartridge shell)

Bernoulli Drives

Iomega Corporation makes a family of drives that use a different principle than SyQuest drives. Instead of a cartridge with a hard disk platter inside, Bernoulli cartridges contain two flexible plastic disks coated with magnetic media. When the disk spins, air flows between the disk's surface and the read/write heads. The reduced air pressure causes the disks to come almost into contact with the heads, yet the air cushion prevents actual contact. This is called the *Bernoulli effect*. Bernoulli drives are highly resistant to vibration and head crashes are virtually unknown. Bernoulli cartridges are a bit more rugged than SyQuest cartridges.

Bernoulli drives come in one form factor (5.25-inch) and five capacities (35, 65, 90, 105, and 150 Mb). The 90 Mb and the 150 Mb are the standard Bernoulli capacities. Bernoulli drives are always seen as external SCSI devices.

This 5.25-inch Bernoulli cartridge can store 150 Mb.

Magneto-Optical Drives

Magneto-optical (MO) drives use a laser to read to and write from a plastic disk. When writing, the laser heats a spot on the disk enough so that it takes on the polarity of a magnet on the other side of the disk. When reading, the disk simply reads the magnetic information on the disk.

The benefits of MO drives are that the cartridges are inexpensive, rugged, hold 128 Mb of data, and are impervious to magnetic fields. There are also 5.25-inch MO drives that use 650 Mb or 1.3 Gb cartridges. MO drives are a good choice for long-term archiving of data.

Magneto-optical drives can be internal or external SCSI devices for the Mac.

A I-3G-b magneto-optical drive (left) and a 128 Mb drive (right).

A 1.3 Gb optical cartridge (left) and a 128 Mb cartridge (right).

REMOVABLE STORAGE COSTS

With so many options for removable storage, you may be feeling a bit over-whelmed. You should consider a few factors before deciding on a drive. First, if you will be exchanging data with someone else, a service bureau for example, ask them what type of cartridges they can accept. This should narrow your options somewhat. Next, you should consider your storage needs. If you will be using the cartridges to transfer or to back up more than 200 Mb of data, you should probably rule out any drive smaller than 100 Mb. Otherwise, you will soon find your office cluttered with cartridges full of data.

Finally, consider the cost. The following three tables show the costs of the media (the cartridges) per megabyte, the cost of the drive itself, and a cost per megabyte combining the cost of the drive and media at various usage levels. We've based these tables on approximate street prices from mail order companies as of this writing; remember that prices change quickly. Use these for comparison and planning, but do your own price checking before you buy.

REMOVABLE MEDIA COSTS.

Cartridge	Capacity (Mb)	Cost	Cost/Mb
Bernoulli	90	$90	$1.00
Bernoulli	150	$100	$0.66
Magneto-optical	128	$45	$0.35
Magneto-optical	1300	$110	$0.08
SyQuest	44	$59	$1.34
SyQuest	88	$78	$0.87
SyQuest	105	$64	$0.61
SyQuest	200	$89	$0.46
SyQuest	270	$95	$0.35

REMOVABLE MEDIA DRIVE COSTS (EXTERNAL UNITS).

Cartridge	Capacity (Mb)	Cost
Bernoulli	90	$370
Bernoulli	150	$480
Magneto-optical	128	$750
Magneto-optical	1300	$2500
SyQuest	44	$230
SyQuest	88	$420
SyQuest	105	$330
SyQuest	200	$500
SyQuest	270	$530

REMOVABLE MEDIA DRIVE'S TOTAL COSTS FOR A GIVEN AMOUNT OF STORAGE (DRIVE PLUS CARTRIDGES).

Cartridge	Capacity (Mb)	Total Storage Costs (in dollars)*					
		100 Mb	200 Mb	300 Mb	500 Mb	1000 Mb	2000 Mb
Bernoulli	90	460	550	640	820	1,360	2,350
Bernoulli	150	480	580	580	780	1,080	1,780
Magneto-optical	128	750	795	840	885	1,065	1,425
Magneto-optical	1300	2,610	2,610	2,610	2,610	2,610	2,720
SyQuest	44	348	466	584	879	1,528	2,885
SyQuest	88	498	576	654	810	1,278	2,136
SyQuest	105	330	394	458	586	906	1,546
SyQuest	200	500	500	589	678	856	1,301
SyQuest	270	530	530	625	625	815	1,195

* All drives come with one cartridge included.

As you can see from the tables, the greater your storage needs, the more economical the larger capacity drives become due to the low cost of the media.

WHAT YOU'LL NEED

Tools aren't necessary to install an external removable cartridge drive. You'll need the following items:

- The removable-cartridge drive and power cord.

- One SCSI cable, either 25-pin to 50-pin (if you're hooking the drive directly to the Mac) or 50-pin to 50-pin (if you're connecting the drive to another SCSI peripheral).

- A SCSI terminator (if the drive is the last device on the SCSI chain).

- The driver software (if any) that came with your drive.

INSTALLING A REMOVABLE-CARTRIDGE DRIVE

To install a removable-cartridge drive, follow these steps:

1 Shut down your Macintosh.

SCSI address switch.

Changing the SCSI address.

2 Check the back of the drive for the SCSI address selector switch. This switch will be a pushbutton or rotary switch.

3 If necessary, change the SCSI address of the drive so that it is different from any of your other SCSI devices. (See Chapter 9, "Hard Drives," if necessary.)

The Mac's SCSI port.

4 Find the SCSI port on the back of your Mac. It has an icon that looks like a diamond with a stick in it, or a stylized letter "G."

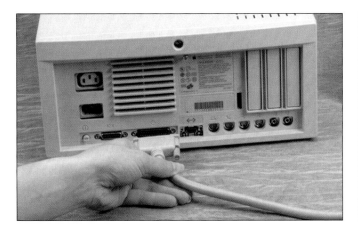

Connecting the SCSI cable to the Mac.

Hooking the SCSI cable to the SyQuest drive.

5 Connect the small end of the SCSI cable to the Mac's SCSI port. Turn the thumbscrews until the cable is secured snugly.

6 Connect the larger end of the SCSI cable to the drive. Snap the wire holders on the drive's SCSI connector inside the ears of the cable's connector.

7 If the drive is the last SCSI device on the SCSI chain, you must attach a SCSI terminator to the other large connector on the back of the drive. If the removable drive is in the middle of the chain, the terminator should be on the last device.

8 Connect the power cable to the drive, and then plug it in.

9 Turn the drive on, insert a cartridge, and then turn on the Mac.

TEST YOUR REMOVABLE-CARTRIDGE DRIVE

Test your new drive by putting a formatted cartridge in the drive and seeing whether the cartridge shows up on your Desktop. If the Mac doesn't recognize the cartridge, check your cables.

An Overview of Scanners

Scanners let you capture an image from a paper and store it as an editable file on your Mac. Most scanners now offer 24-bit color capability (that means they can scan millions of colors) and also can scan grayscale images, line art, and text. Scanners are inexpensive, too; many good scanners now sell for less than $1,000.

A scanner moves a bright light, called a *scanning head,* across a page and measures the amount of light being reflected from the page. The reflections are read by the scanner as a group of finely spaced dots. The *resolution,* or density of the dots in the image, is measured by the number of *dots per inch* (dpi). The majority of scanners in the $1,000 price range scan at resolutions of 300 dpi or 600 dpi. 300 dpi resolution is fine for line art and scanned images that will be printed on office laser printers or on newsprint. Higher resolutions are necessary for good reproduction of photographs and for most professional printing. Some scanners attempt to get higher resolutions through *interpolation.* This increases the apparent resolution of scanned images by using software to add dots between those actually "seen" by the scanner and to estimate their color. Interpolation doesn't enable the scanner to pick up detail that's smaller than what it can see, but it does smooth jagged edges.

In addition to scanning artwork, many scanners are used for *Optical Character Recognition* (OCR), which captures a page of text and converts it into editable text on the Mac. Without OCR, you will receive only a graphic image of the page. Most scanners come with image scanning software, but OCR software must be purchased separately. OCR software can range from $99 up to thousands of dollars. Low-cost OCR software has limited capabilities; typically, the low-cost OCR is limited in the number of type fonts that it can successfully recognize and requires pages to be typographically simple, like a sheet of typewritten text. The more expensive software can read complex pages with multiple columns and different type sizes and fonts.

Most image scanning software bundled with scanners comes in the form of a *plug-in,* a software component that adds features—in this case the ability to use the scanner—to Adobe Photoshop, Fractal Design's Painter, Micro-Frontier's ColorIt, and many other popular image-editing applications that can use plug-ins. Other scanning software is in the form of an application. The best known is LightSource's Ofoto, which is smart enough to automatically fix some problems with original artwork. For example, Ofoto can automatically straighten crooked artwork and adjust the scan for optimum brightness and contrast. An important standard for scanners comes from Apple, with its ColorSync color-management extension for System 7. ColorSync is a system that attempts to provide device-independent correct color so that a scan made with one scanner will come out with the same color values as the same scan made on another scanner. ColorSync also works with monitors so that a particular image will look the same on different monitors.

An external Apple OneScanner.

Lid

Scanning stage

WHAT YOU'LL NEED

Tools aren't usually necessary to install a scanner. You'll need the following items:

- The scanner.

- One SCSI cable, either 25-pin to 50-pin (if you're hooking the scanner directly to the Mac) or 50-pin to 50-pin (if you're connecting the scanner to another SCSI peripheral).

- A SCSI terminator (if the scanner is the last device on the SCSI chain).

- The scanning software that came bundled with your scanner.

INSTALLING A SCANNER

1 Shut down your Macintosh.

2 Many scanners come with their scanning heads locked down for shipment to prevent possible damage. Check the scanner's documentation to see if you have to unlock or release the scanning head.

3 Check the back of the scanner for the SCSI address selector switch. This will be a pushbutton or a rotary switch.

Rotary SCSI address switch.   *Pushbutton SCSI address switch.*

4 If necessary, change the SCSI address of the scanner so that it is different from any of your other SCSI devices. (See Chapter 9, "Hard Drives," for details on setting SCSI addresses.)

Note: The SCSI chain on most Macs can have up to seven devices on it. Each device must have a unique address on the SCSI chain and the allowable addresses are from 0 to 7. The Macintosh is always set at address 7; the internal hard drive is usually set at address 0. This leaves you with six addresses to use with other hard drives, CD-ROM drives, or scanners.

The SCSI port on the back of the Mac.

5 Locate the SCSI port on the back of your Mac. It has an icon that looks like a diamond with a stick in it, or a really stylized letter "G."

Connecting the SCSI cable to the SCSI port on the back of the Mac.

6 Connect the small end of the SCSI cable to the Mac's SCSI port. Turn the thumbscrews until the cable is secured.

Hooking the SCSI cable to the scanner.

7 Connect the larger (50-pin) end of the SCSI cable to the scanner. Snap the wire holders on the scanner's SCSI connector inside the ears of the cable's connector.

The SCSI cable and terminator on the scanner.

SCSI terminator

8 If the scanner is the last SCSI device on the SCSI chain, you must attach a SCSI terminator to the other large connector on the back of the scanner. If the scanner is in the middle of the chain, the terminator should be on the last device.

9 Plug the scanner in, turn the scanner on, and then turn on the Mac. Install the scanning software that came with your scanner by following the instructions included with the software.

TEST YOUR SCANNER

Test your new acquisition by following the directions that came with the scanner. If the scanner doesn't work, check the following:

- Did you unlock the scanner's scanning head? Check the scanner's manual for specific instructions on how this is done.

- Is the unit plugged in and turned on?

- Are the SCSI cables attached securely?

- Is the SCSI chain terminated?

- Is the scanning software installed properly?

CHAPTER

14

Printers

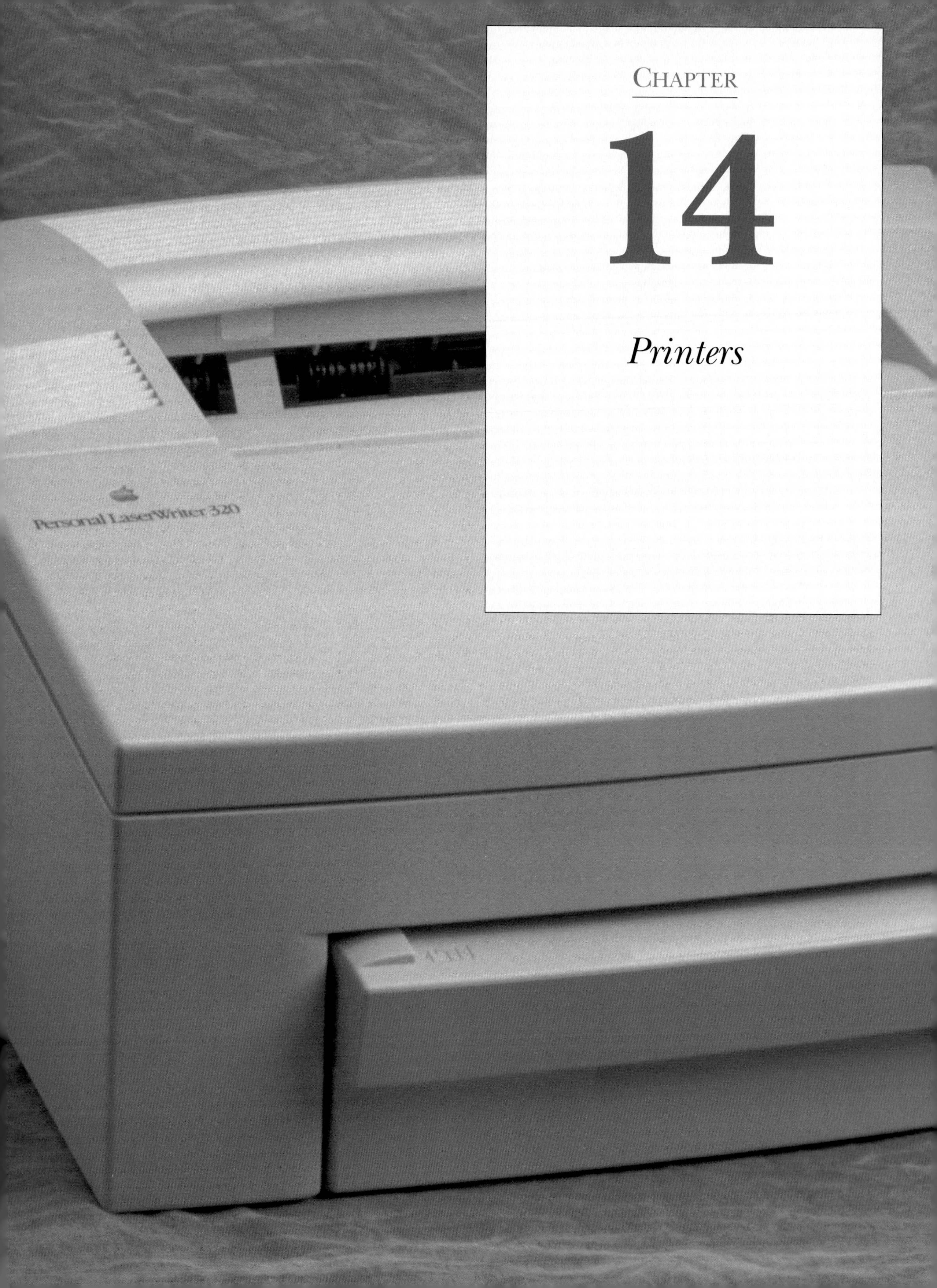

AN OVERVIEW OF PRINTERS

The most common reason for upgrading a printer is that your old printer just died. Sadly, it's often the case that it is more cost-effective to replace a broken printer than it is to repair it, especially if the printer is more than a couple of years old. Because the printer is a mechanical (as opposed to digital) device, wear and tear take a heavy toll.

Printers for the Mac generally fall into one of four categories:

- Dot-matrix
- Inkjet
- Color inkjet
- Laser

An Apple StyleWriter II inkjet printer.

An Apple Personal LaserWriter 320 laser printer.

Dot-matrix printers use a print head made up of a series of vertically aligned pins that strike the ribbon, paper, and platen as the print head moves from left to right. These pins create an array of dots that make up the printed characters. Dot-matrix printers are useful for printing multipart forms, such as invoices. There was a time when dot-matrix printers were the most economical printing solution. However, inkjet prices are now lower than those for dot-matrix, and the quality of the inkjet is higher. Unless you need to print multipart forms, a dot-matrix printer is not the best solution. Very few dot-matrix printers are created specifically for the Mac, with the notable exception of the venerable Apple ImageWriter II. However, hundreds of PC dot-matrix printers can be used with the Macintosh by using GDT Softworks' PowerPrint. This package contains a serial-to-parallel conversion cable and a set of printer drivers that cover many makes of PC dot-matrix, laser, and inkjet printers.

Inkjet printers work in somewhat the same fashion as dot-matrix printers. Instead of pins hitting a ribbon, however, inkjets spray ink dots through tiny nozzles onto the paper. Color inkjets work the same way, though they use ink reservoirs, each filled with one of three or four colors (black, yellow, cyan, and magenta).

Laser printers are a close cousin to the copy machine. Like copiers, laser printers electrostatically charge a drum in patterns. The drum picks up toner, deposits the toner in the patterns onto the paper, and then thermally fuses the toner to the paper.

Most laser printers used with the Macintosh are PostScript printers, which means that they contain a processor that uses Adobe Systems' PostScript page description language. PostScript allows printers to print fonts and images at any size with the full resolution of the printing device. For example, you could print the same page from a page layout program to two PostScript printers, one a 300 dpi (dots per inch) and the other a 600 dpi. A PostScript printer contains its own RAM and processor, so it handles the steps necessary to make the image print well on either printer.

CHOOSING A PRINTER

You'll need to weigh several factors when choosing a new printer. The first consideration should be for you to have a clear idea of what you need the printer to accomplish. For example, if you rarely print and just need a printer for the occasional letter, chances are that an inkjet printer will do the job. If you need to print on multipart forms, you have to get a dot-matrix printer. People who generate a lot of printed copy will require a laser printer. Users who work with graphics and desktop publishing will find that a PostScript laser printer is a must. And if you need to generate presentations as well as text, a color inkjet might be the best choice for you.

The next consideration will be the amount of money you have to spend. In every category of printer, there's a wide spread of prices and capabilities.

You'll need to juggle the tradeoff between features and price to choose the right printer for you.

WHAT YOU'LL NEED

Tools aren't necessary to install printers or their consumables. You'll need the following items:

- The printer and its power cable.
- The printer cable or network connectors.
- A printer ribbon, ink cartridge, or toner cartridge, depending on the type of printer you're installing.
- Printer driver software that came with the printer (if any).

INSTALLING A NEW PERSONAL PRINTER

To install your personal printer, follow these steps:

1 Shut down your Macintosh.

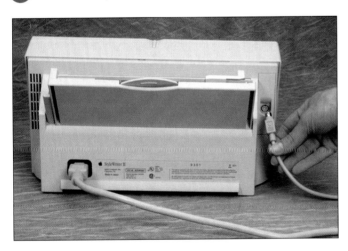

Plugging the cable into the printer.

The Mac's printer port.

2 Take the printer cable and plug one end of it into the port on the printer.

3 Find the round printer port on the back of your Macintosh. It's the one with the icon of a printer by it.

The completed
printer connection.

4 Plug the other end of the printer cable into the printer port. Plug the power cable that came with the printer into the back of the printer, and then into the wall outlet or your plug strip.

5 Install the printer driver software that came with your printer in the Mac's System Folder. To do this, insert the floppy disk with the driver software into your Mac. Double-click the icon of the disk to open it, and then drag the icon of the printer driver to your Mac's System Folder. Click OK when the Mac asks if it is all right to install the driver into your Extensions folder.

INSTALLING A NETWORKED PRINTER

Laser printers are often expensive, and in an office environment it's an advantage for several Macintoshes to share one. The most common way to connect the Macs to the printer is to use the LocalTalk networking software built into every Macintosh. LocalTalk is a fairly low-speed networking system that is inexpensive to install and a snap to maintain. It is ideal for sharing a printer, or for light file transfers between computers with System 7's File Sharing.

LocalTalk hardware is available from Apple and many other vendors. The most popular LocalTalk connectors are Farallon's PhoneNET connectors. These connectors use regular RJ-11 phone wires with modular plugs as the network wire, which makes setting up a LocalTalk network cheap and fast. Several other companies make LocalTalk connectors that are interchangable with Farallon's (and less expensive), so when you shop, you should look for the best deal. To create a network, you need one PhoneNET-type connector for each device on the network. So if you have five Macs that you want to hook up to one printer, you'll need six PhoneNET-type connectors, one for each Mac and one for the printer.

Hooking up a printer to PhoneNET is easy. Follow these steps (we've used a Personal LaserWriter 320 here, but your printer should be similar):

A Farallon PhoneNET connector.

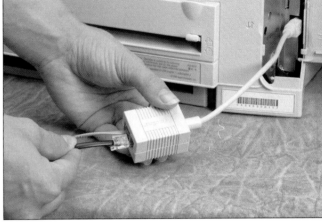

Connecting a RJ-11 cable.

1 Turn the printer off.

Getting at the network connector.

2 On the back of the printer, open the door to expose the network connector.

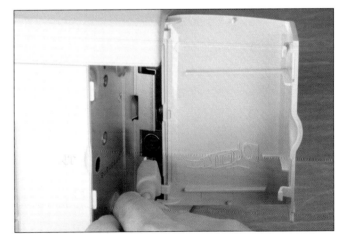

Plugging the PhoneNET connector into the printer's LocalTalk port.

3 Plug one PhoneNET connector into the LocalTalk port on the back of the printer.

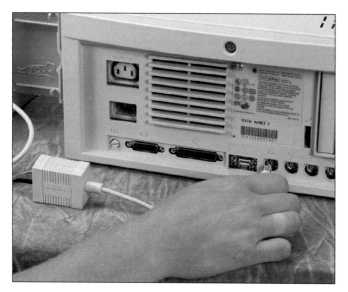

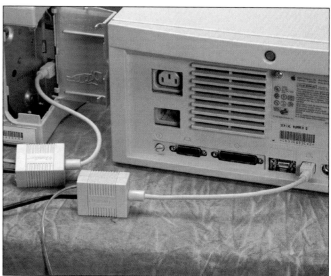

Plugging in the PhoneNET connector.

The completed printer network connection.

4 Plug another PhoneNET connector into the printer port on the back of the Macintosh.

5 Connect the PhoneNET connectors with an RJ-11 cable plugged into each connector.

6 Each PhoneNET connector has two jacks. If the PhoneNET connector is at the end of the network chain, plug a phone line terminating plug into the open jack. (The terminator looks like an RJ-11 plug with a small looped wire instead of a phone line.) If there is another computer on the chain, plug another RJ-11 cable into the open jack to connect to the other computer.

7 Plug the printer's power cord into the wall outlet or your power strip. Turn on the printer and your Mac, and then install the printer driver software that came with your printer into the Mac's System Folder. To do this, insert the floppy disk with the driver software into your Mac. Double-click the icon of the disk to open it, and then drag the icon of the printer driver to your Mac's System Folder. Click OK when the Mac asks if it is all right to install the driver into your Extensions folder.

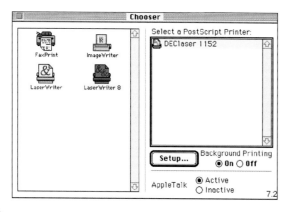

Selecting the printer in the Chooser.

8 Go to the Chooser (it's in the Apple menu). Click the AppleTalk Active radio button at the bottom of the window.

9 Restart your Macintosh.

10 When the Mac has booted, open the Chooser again. At the left side of the window, click the LaserWriter icon to select it. The name of your printer should appear at the right side of the Chooser window. Click the printer name to select that printer. Close the Chooser window.

REPLACING AN INK CARTRIDGE (INKJET PRINTERS)

Adding an ink cartridge to an inkjet printer is a quick and clean task. Here's how to change the cartridge for a StyleWriter II (most other inkjets are similar):

1 Turn the printer off.

A new StyleWriter cartridge.

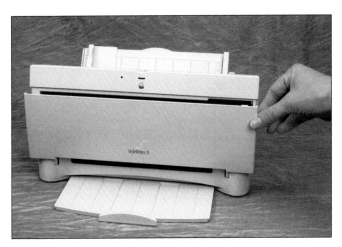

Getting at the print mechanism.

2 Remove the new ink cartridge from its packaging; then remove the orange tape and orange cap from the cartridge.

3 Open the door on the front of the StyleWriter II to expose the print mechanism.

Push up on this lever.

Unlocking the ink cartridge.

Removing the old ink cartridge.

4 Press the blue cartridge locking lever next to the ink cartridge up until it unlocks.

5 Pull the old cartridge out of the StyleWriter.

Installing the new cartridge.

6 Insert the new cartridge into the printer. The label should be towards you.

Locking the cartridge into place.

7 Once the new cartridge is seated in its cradle, press down on the blue locking lever to secure the cartridge.

8 Close the door on the front of the printer, and then turn on the printer. The StyleWriter II will prime the new cartridge, which takes about 15 seconds.

REPLACING A TONER CARTRIDGE (LASER PRINTERS)

Changing the toner cartridge in a laser printer is an easy task. Follow these steps:

1 Turn off the printer.

Opening the laser printer.

2 Open the top or front of your printer. (Different models do this in different ways. Check the manual for your printer if you're unsure.)

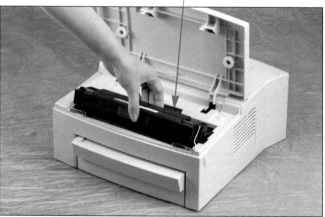

The toner cartridge

Removing the old toner cartridge.

3 If there is a toner cartridge already in the printer, remove it by pulling it up and out.

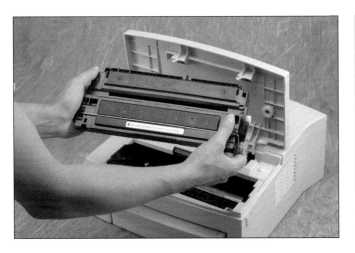

Rocking the toner cartridge.

4 Take the replacement cartridge out of its box. The toner inside the new cartridge may have settled during shipment; you should gently rock the cartridge to distribute the toner evenly. Be sure to rock it front to back, not end to end.

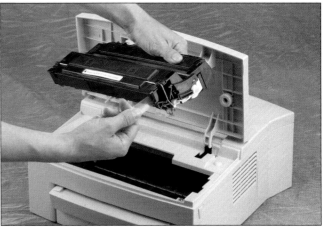

Removing the cartridge seal.

5 Remove the seal that is in place on the new cartridge. Different models of toner cartridges have different types of seals; you should check the instructions that came with the cartridge to see where the seal is and how to remove it.

Sliding the new cartridge in.

6 Install the new cartridge by sliding it down and into the printer. When it is seated properly, close the front or top of the printer, turn it on, and print a test page.

TROUBLESHOOTING

If your printer doesn't work, check the following:

- Are the cables secure?
- Does the printer have paper in it?
- Have you installed the correct printer driver for your printer into the Mac's System Folder?
- Have you picked your printer in the Mac's chooser?
- If you're using a networked printer, is AppleTalk active? Look in the Chooser if you're not sure.
- Does your laser printer's output have vertical streaks running the length of the page? If so, this usually means a defective toner cartridge. Replace it and try again.

AN OVERVIEW OF MODEMS

So you want to get connected and get online? First, you'll need a modem. Unfortunately, it's not always easy to figure out which features you need. There's an alphabet soup of abbreviations and acronyms for modem standards and protocols; it's enough to make your head spin. Here's a primer that should get you in and out of the store with the least amount of hassle and confusion.

First of all, what's a modem? The word stands for MOdulator/DEModulator; it's a device that modulates, or converts, the digital signal from your computer into a series of tones and other sounds that are sent over the phone line. On the other end, the receiving modem demodulates the tones back into a digital form that the other computer can understand. Modems transmit data at standardized speeds; these speeds are expressed in *bits per second* (bps). With bps speeds, the higher and faster, the better. The speeds we're concerned with are 2400 bps, 9600 bps, and 14,400 bps. Slower speeds are yesterday's news, and you shouldn't even consider a 1200 bps modem. The advantage of a faster modem is better performance when receiving a file or other information from online services such as CompuServe, America Online, or Prodigy. These services charge by the minute; time online is literally money. There are some exceptions, but generally speaking, the faster you can get your work done, the cheaper it is for you. The first principle in buying a modem is to get the fastest modem you can afford. It's most likely you'll end up with a 9600 bps or 14,400 bps modem, as those are the main types of modems sold today.

When you shop, you're likely to run across the terms *V.32* and *V.32bis*. These are the official names for the international standards for 9600 bps and 14,400 bps communications, respectively. Most online services now have local 9600 bps and 14,400 bps dial-up numbers in major cities. You can buy faster modems; the V.32TERBO modem transmits at 19,200 bps, but it isn't a widely accepted modem standard. It was an interim standard adopted by a few modem manufacturers while they were waiting for the speedier V.FAST standard to be approved. You should pass on a V.32TERBO modem. V.FAST is the up-and-coming, internationally-approved standard for the blazing 28,800 bps modems, and it will be the standard of the future, though there aren't many online places that use it today. V.FAST modems are about twice the price of a V.32bis unit.

Static and noise on a phone line can distort a stream of data and prevent information from being sent correctly. It's possible to control errors on phone lines with correction schemes based in the modem hardware. The most popular of these error-correction standards are called *MNP levels 2-4* and *V.42*. Because reliable connections prevent user frustration due to garbled data, V.42 compliance is another item to add to your modem buying checklist. Another feature to look for in a modem is *data compression*. This, in effect, squashes the data stream so that it takes less space and less time to transmit over the phone. The data compression standards to look for are V.42bis and MNP 5.

When you're buying a modem, you'll be faced with another decision: do you want to send and/or receive faxes from your computer? If you do, you'll want a fax modem. Fax modem hardware and software have changed in the past couple of years. Fax modems used to be buggy and clumsy to use. Now, however, faxing is almost as easy as printing. If you already have a regular fax machine, a fax modem might seem like a luxury. But, if you're printing your documents now, only to feed them into your fax machine, a fax modem saves time and paper. Because most modems include fax capability for little extra cost, why not have a fax modem? Even if you only use the fax features occasionally, it's worth the convenience.

Here's a checklist of items that you should get when shopping for a modem:

- 9600 bps (V.32) or 14,400 bps (V.32bis) data transmission

- V.42 error correction

- Both V.42bis and MNP 5 data compression

- 9600 bps or 14,400 bps send-and receive fax-capability

The vast majority of modems for the desktop Macintosh are external units. A few manufacturers have introduced internal modems, but they are not popular among Mac users, with the exception of PowerBook modems.

An external modem can come in almost any size and shape, but the one shown below is typical. It has a power switch on the front, and several indicator lights that flash when the modem is in use and give information about what the modem is doing. For example, when the modem is sending data, the SD light flashes; the RD light blinks when the modem is receiving data.

A typical external modem.

Power switch

Indicator lights

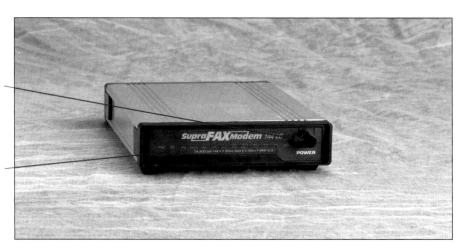

On the back of the same modem, you'll find the connector jacks for data, power, and two phone jacks. The wire from one jack goes to the wall, and the other jack lets you plug your telephone into the modem. By having your phone plugged into your modem, you can use the computer and modem to dial the phone for you.

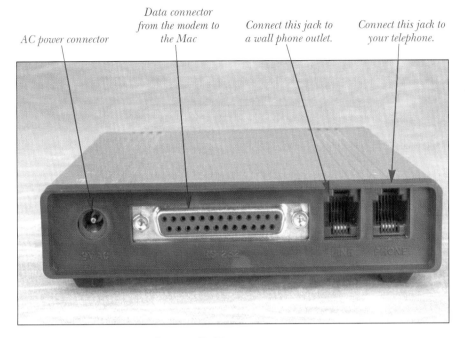

AC power connector

Data connector from the modem to the Mac

Connect this jack to a wall phone outlet.

Connect this jack to your telephone.

The modem's rear panel.

WHAT YOU'LL NEED

Tools aren't usually necessary to install an external modem. You might need a small flat-blade screwdriver for some serial cables. You'll need the following items:

- The modem.

- A standard phone cable (also called an RJ-11 cable, after the name of the connector at each end of the cable). Your modem probably comes with one of these. You'll need two of these if you plan to use a phone with the modem too.

- A modem data cable. This cable has a 25-pin serial plug on one end and a Mac serial plug with a DIN-8 connector that plugs into the modem port on the back of your Mac. This cable may come with your modem

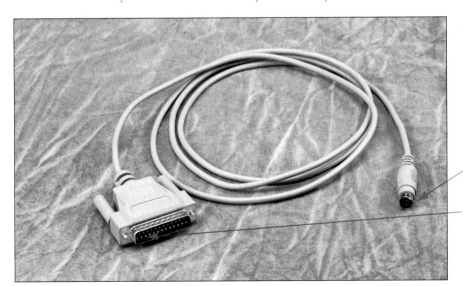

A modem data cable transmits information between the modem and your Mac.

This end connects to the Mac.

This end connects to the modem.

INSTALLING THE MODEM

To install your modem, follow these steps:

Connecting the RJ-11 cable to the LINE jack on the modem.   *The RJ-11 cable in place.*

1 Plug the phone cable into the jack on the back of the modem labeled LINE or WALL. If you want to hook your phone to your modem, you can plug the wire that runs from your phone into the jack on the back of the modem labeled PHONE. Don't panic if your modem has two unlabeled phone jacks on its rear panel; some newer modems can use either jack for the phone or the wall outlet.

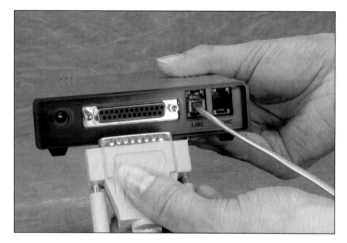

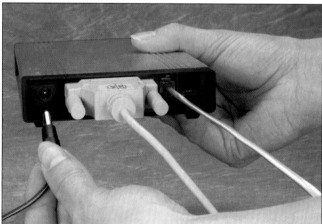

Attaching the serial data cable to the modem.   *Connecting the modem's power cable.*

2 Next, plug the modem data cable into the wide female 25-pin serial port on the back of the modem. Most modem data cables have thumbscrews that you can tighten to secure the cable. A few cables may use small screws instead of the thumbscrews. If you have one of these, use a small

flat-blade screwdriver to secure the cable to the back of the modem.

3 Plug the DC power connector from the modem's AC adapter into the back of the modem. Plug the AC adapter into the wall or a power strip.

The modem port on the back of a Mac.

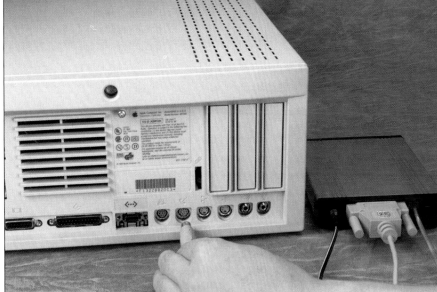

Plugging the data cable into the Macintosh.

4 Find the modem port on the back of the Macintosh. It has an icon of a phone receiver with bits of data streaming from it.

5 Plug the other end of the data cable into the Mac's modem port. The flat side of the connector or the side with an arrow goes on top.

6 Turn on your Mac and your modem, install your communications software, and get out onto the Information Superhighway.

TEST YOUR MODEM

Your modem probably came bundled with a simple terminal program, which is one kind of software that can talk to a modem. Check the manual that came with the terminal program if necessary, and then do these steps to make sure your Mac is connected to the modem correctly:

1. Start your terminal program.

2. Type the following command, and then press the Return key:

   atdt

This command tells the modem to take the phone line off the hook. You should hear a dial tone and the computer screen should respond with OK. Press any key to hang up the phone line. If you don't hear the dial tone or get the OK response, check to make sure that you've installed the modem hardware and the communications software correctly.

An Overview of External Speakers

Every Macintosh has a built-in speaker for system sounds, and some are a fairly good quality. But if you're working with digitized music, QuickTime movies, CD-ROM based games, or multimedia applications, you'll want to upgrade the fidelity of your sound output. The solution is to invest in a pair of powered external speakers. These plug into the sound port on the back of your Mac and give you high-quality, stereo sound (if your Mac outputs stereo; if not, you'll get mono output). You'll probably want to place one speaker on either side of your monitor. Some computer speakers are actually designed to attach to your monitor and to sound best when you're only a few feet away from the speakers. They're called *powered* speakers because they contain a small amplifier that boosts your Mac's sound output, and they need to be plugged into AC power to drive this amplifier. You'll usually find volume and tone controls on one or both of the speakers.

It's possible to use the kind of powered speakers that are sold as add-ons for portable stereos, but it's not the best solution. Speakers are basically electromagnets, and their magnetic field can affect your computer, monitor, peripherals, or even floppy disks. You're better off buying *shielded speakers,* which have a special interior lining to prevent magnetic distortion. Look for speakers with the designation of "multimedia" or "computer," and then check with the dealer to make sure that they're shielded.

Apple sells the AppleDesign Powered Speakers II, which are a good choice, but a tad expensive. They're a better value when bundled with an Apple CD300 Plus CD-ROM drive; the combination is called the Apple Multimedia Kit. Other good picks in powered speakers come from Yamaha, Bose, Altec Lansing, Labtec, and Persona Technologies.

Powered external computer speakers.

Volume and tone controls

Apple has included stereo speakers with some of its products. One, the Apple AudioVision 14 Display, is designed for use as a personal multimedia workstation. The AudioVision 14 Display has two stereo speakers, a 14-inch Trinitron monitor, and a directional microphone for voice annotation (some programs, like Microsoft Word, allow you to add voice notes to documents) or speech recognition (which lets some Macs be controlled by your vocal commands). The display also has video and sound input jacks on its sides.

The Apple AudioVision 14 Display is a good choice for personal multimedia.

Microphone

Stereo speakers

Volume control

Some Macs in the Performa and LC lines, notably the Performa 575, have built-in stereo speakers.

If even a good set of computer speakers doesn't produce the quality of sound you are looking for, you can connect the speaker output of your Mac to a stereo amplifier's input. To do this, you need a stereo mini-headphone plug RCA adapter cord (shown below). The mini-headphone plug end plugs into the Mac speaker output and the RCA plug end plugs into your stereo amp's input. This should give you the same sound quality through your stereo speakers as any other device, such as a CD player or tape deck, you use with it.

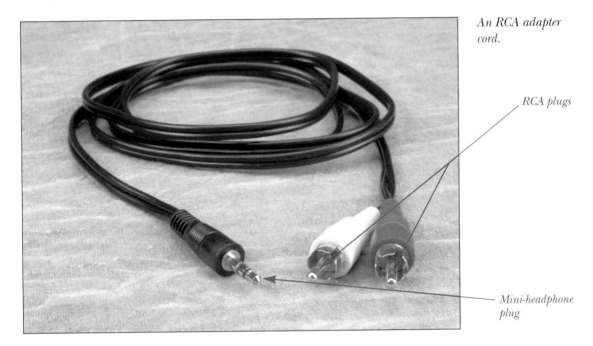

An RCA adapter cord.

RCA plugs

Mini-headphone plug

WHAT YOU'LL NEED

Tools aren't usually necessary to install external speakers. All you should need are your Mac and the new speakers.

INSTALLING EXTERNAL SPEAKERS

To install internal speakers, follow these steps:

1 Shut down your Macintosh.

*Connecting the
secondary speaker.*

2 Depending on the model of speakers you use, one of the them will be the primary speaker, and the other will be the secondary speaker. Usually the primary speaker contains the amplifier and the power input jack. Find the cable that runs from the primary speaker to the secondary speaker. Plug this cable into the jack on the back of the secondary speaker.

*The sound output
connector looks the
same on every Mac
model.*

3 Find the sound output connector on the back of your Macintosh. It's the one with the icon of a speaker above it.

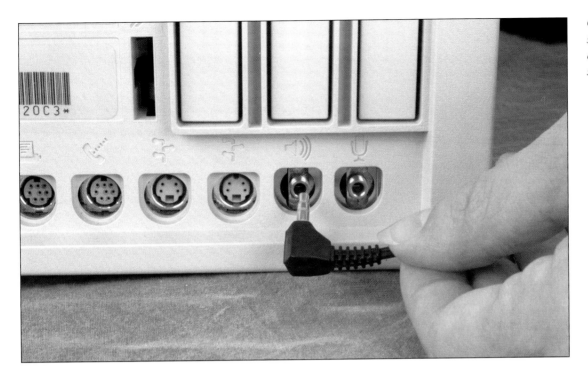

Connecting the speaker's input cable to the Mac's sound output.

4 Plug the input cable from the primary speaker into the Mac's sound output connector.

5 Connect the speaker's power supply to the primary speaker, and then plug the power supply into an AC outlet. Turn on the speakers and start your Macintosh. Enjoy the improved sound!

TROUBLESHOOTING

If you don't hear anything from your new speakers, check for one of the following possibilities:

- Make sure that the speakers are connected to AC power and each other, and turned on. Adjust the volume controls on the speakers if needed.

- Check that the Mac's sound output is turned up. Check in the Sound control panel to make sure that the volume slider isn't set for zero.

- Check to see if you plugged the speakers into the sound *input* jack (it has an icon like a microphone) by mistake. If so, switch the plug to the correct jack.

- Some external speakers run on batteries rather than an AC electrical plug. Check any instructions that came with your speakers to see if they need batteries. If they do, be sure the batteries are charged and correctly inserted.

Keyboards, Mice, and Trackballs

An Overview of Keyboards, Mice, and Trackballs

Input devices are the main way that you communicate with your Macintosh. Unless you're using voice commands with one of the AV Macs or the Power Macs, you'll use a keyboard, and either a mouse or a trackball to control your computer.

All of the input devices connect to each other and to the Mac itself using a low-speed bus called the Apple Desktop Bus, or ADB for short. ADB devices are daisy-chained together, and you can have as many as eight ADB devices in the chain, though two or three is the norm. You connect ADB devices together by simply plugging their cables into an ADB port, either on a Mac or another ADB peripheral. The port and the cable will have matching ADB icons; just orient the flat portion of the ADB connector to match the flat part of the ADB port, and plug the cable in.

The ADB chain connecting a Mac Classic II, a regular keyboard, and a mouse.

ADB cables

The ADB port on a Mac.

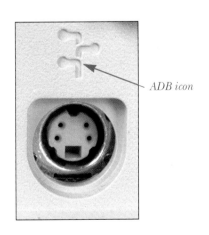

ADB icon

KEYBOARDS

An Apple standard keyboard.

An Apple Extended Keyboard.

The two most common keyboards are the Apple standard keyboard, which includes a numeric keypad; and the Apple Extended Keyboard, which has a numeric keypad plus a number of function keys. Because most Mac software doesn't take advantage of these extra keys, you'll need to buy a macro program, such as CE Software's QuicKeys or Affinity's Tempo II Plus, to get the most out of the function keys.

*An Apple
Adjustable
Keyboard.*

Typing on keyboards for hours at a time can cause injury. The act of repeating the same motions without sufficient rest creates a condition that can affect the hands, wrists, arms, and back, called Repetitive Strain Injury, or RSI. RSI is a serious and painful problem for thousands of people; in extreme cases, people lose the function of their hands and take years to heal. In an attempt to address the RSI problem, Apple produces the Apple Adjustable Keyboard. It has integral wrist rests and a separate numeric keypad with function keys. The main keyboard is hinged in the middle, splitting so that your hands can rest on the keyboard in a more natural fashion, rather than having to tuck your elbows in close to your sides as with traditional keyboards.

Mice

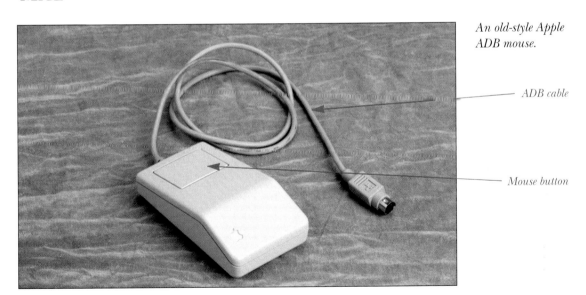

*An old-style Apple
ADB mouse.*

— *ADB cable*

— *Mouse button*

A modern Apple ADB mouse.

ADB cable

Mouse button

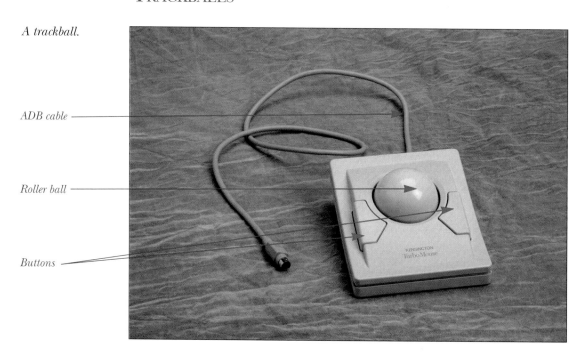

A mouse comes with every Macintosh, and it's unlikely that you'll be upgrading it. Using the mouse is integral to the Macintosh experience. You use it to point at icons, select text, and drag items on the Desktop.

TRACKBALLS

A trackball.

ADB cable

Roller ball

Buttons

A *trackball* is another pointing device. In effect, a trackball is a mouse turned upside down, with the roller ball on the top. A trackball remains stationary on your desk, and you use your fingers to roll the roller ball in its cradle. Trackballs often have two buttons; the software supplied with the trackball can give one or both of the buttons special capabilities. For example, one button can act as a regular mouse button, while the other acts as a click lock for easy dragging, as though you were holding down the mouse button and dragging. Trackballs are good for people with limited desk space, and they're essential in most PowerBooks. Trackballs are an inexpensive addition to your system, but make sure that you try before you buy; some people love using trackballs, and other people hate using them.

Other than replacing a mouse with a trackball, there's not much upgrading to do with input devices. It's important, however, to maintain them, and the best way to keep them running well is regular cleaning.

WHAT YOU'LL NEED

Cleaning input devices is a low-tech affair. Some manufacturers make a small vacuum cleaner designed to suck dirt out of keyboards, but it is not usually necessary. Most of the time, the only tools you need are common household items.

- A clean, soft cotton cloth

- Cotton swabs

- Rubbing alcohol

- Toothpicks

- Spray glass cleaner

- Can of compressed air (optional)

CLEANING THE KEYBOARD

Keyboards pick up dust from the air, and oil and grime from your fingers. Long-neglected keyboards can even gum up one or more keys, making it difficult or impossible to use the keyboard. Avoid this by following these cleaning steps regularly:

 Shut down your Macintosh and unplug, at the keyboard end, the ADB cable that runs from your Mac to the keyboard.

> **Note:** Apple recommends that you turn your Mac off before you connect or disconnect any of your cables. While many people have gotten away with it for years, Apple claims that plugging in an ADB device while the Mac is on can possibly burn out the ADB controller chip on the motherboard, necessitating an expensive repair. Don't take that chance; turn your Mac off before you remove or install any ADB device.

2 Using the cloth, dust the keyboard. If there are any stubborn deposits of grime that won't come off with gentle rubbing, moisten the cloth with one spray of the glass cleaner, and then try again. Never spray the glass cleaner directly onto the keyboard. If you have a can of compressed air, give the keyboard a few blasts to blow out the dust that's gathered below the keyboard's surface. The nooks and crannies of the keyboard can be cleaned with a dry cotton swab, if necessary.

3 Reconnect the ADB cable to the keyboard, start up your Mac, and type away!

CLEANING THE MOUSE

Rolling around on your desktop or mouse pad, a mouse can pick up dirt that eventually gums up its internal rollers, making your on-screen pointer track incorrectly. Follow these steps to keep your mouse in top shape:

1 Shut down your Macintosh.

The roller ball   *The locking ring*

The bottom of a mouse.

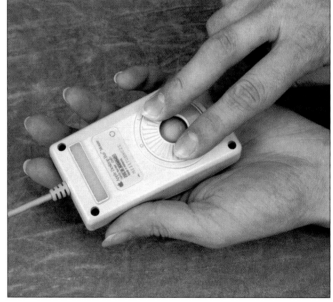

Turning the locking ring.

2 Turn the mouse over. Holding the mouse in one hand, use your other hand to turn the locking ring on the bottom of the mouse counterclockwise about a quarter turn.

A roller with encrusted dirt

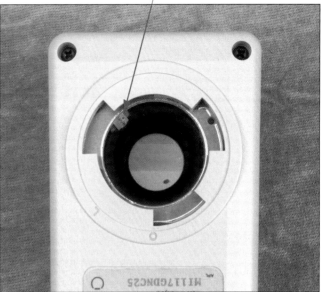

Removing the roller ball.

A dirty mouse.

3 When the locking ring is disengaged, the ring and roller ball should fall out onto your palm. Put them aside for now. Make sure that the ball doesn't fall on the floor or become damaged; it needs to remain perfectly round in order to work correctly.

Cleaning the mouse's rollers.

4 Using a cotton swab moistened with the rubbing alcohol (that's moistened, not soaked) wipe the rollers inside the mouse clean. You may need to scrape the rollers with a toothpick to remove stubborn dirt.

5 Roll the roller ball in a clean, lint-free cloth. Never use rubbing alcohol on the roller ball, as alcohol can ruin the ball's rubber surface.

6 Make sure that the inside of the mouse is dry, and place the roller ball back in the mouse. Put the locking ring on, aligning the tabs on the locking ring with the slots in the bottom of the mouse. Then turn it clockwise about a quarter turn until the ring locks into place.

CLEANING THE TRACKBALL

Because a trackball is, in effect, a mouse turned upside down, cleaning the trackball is almost exactly like cleaning a mouse. Follow these steps:

1 Shut down your Macintosh.

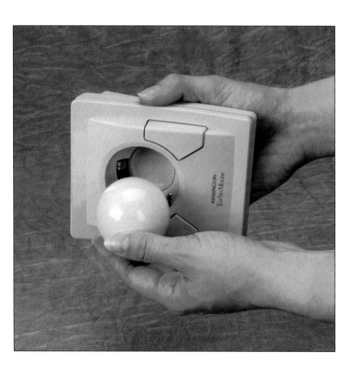

Removing the roller ball from the trackball.

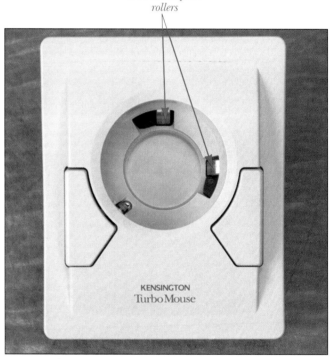

Dirt buildup on rollers

A dirty trackball.

2 Cup one hand over the ball and turn the trackball over. The roller ball will fall out into your hand.

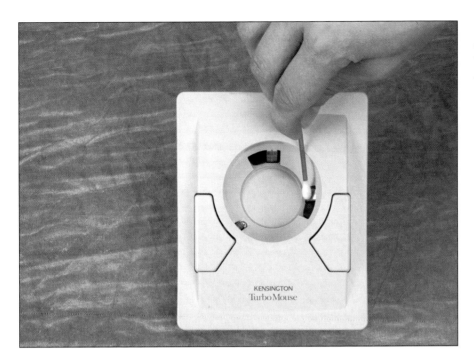

Cleaning the trackball rollers with a cotton swab.

3 Using a cotton swab lightly moistened with the rubbing alcohol, wipe the rollers inside the trackball clean. You may need to scrape the rollers with a toothpick to remove stubborn dirt.

4 Roll the roller ball in a clean, lint-free cloth.

5 Make sure that the inside of the trackball is dry, and place the roller ball back in.

TROUBLESHOOTING

Mice, keyboards, and trackballs are very reliable devices. If one of them stops working, chances are the problem is one of the following:

- If your Mac starts up normally, but the mouse and keyboard don't work, you probably have a loose ADB cable. Check the connection at the back of your Mac and along the ADB chain.

- If your on-screen cursor starts tracking only in a horizontal or vertical direction, try cleaning your mouse. If the problem persists, one of the sensors inside the mouse has probably gone bad. Unfortunately, you'll have to replace the mouse. This goes for trackballs, too.

- If you have just one sticky key on the keyboard, the key mechanism is probably gummed up. Shut the Mac down, unplug the keyboard, and pry off the cap of the sticky key. Then treat the key shaft to a few sprays with some aerosol contact cleaner, available in most electronics stores. Work the shaft up and down while you spray. If this doesn't work, you'll have to take the keyboard in for repair.

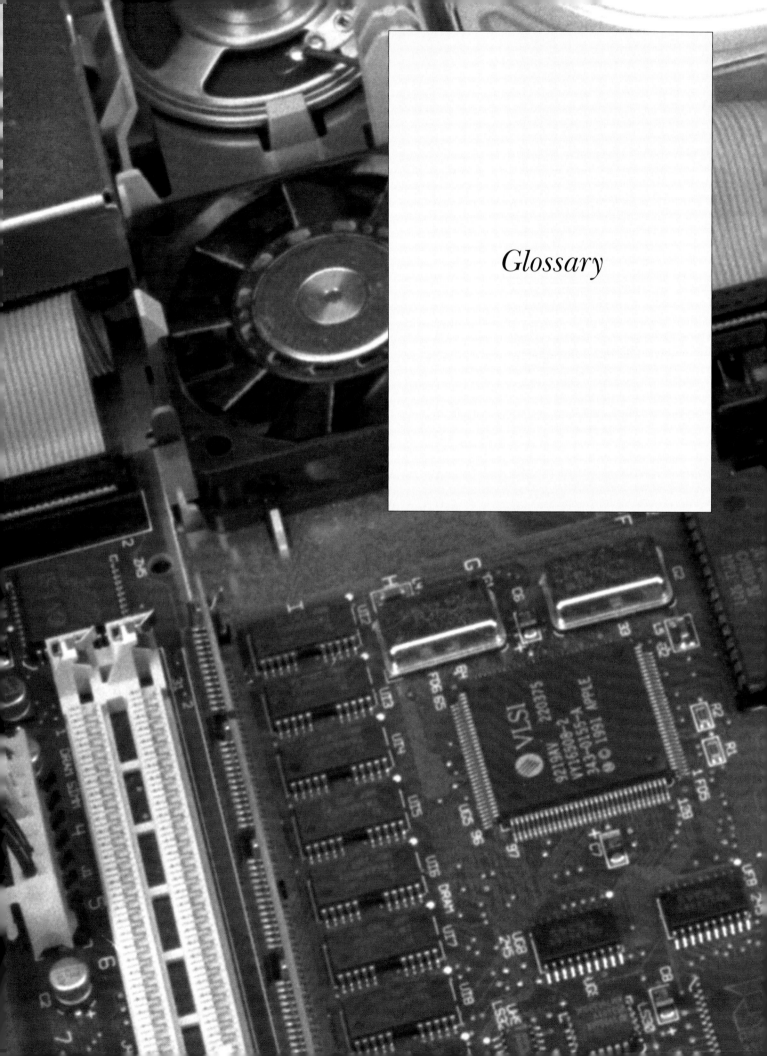

Glossary

64K ROM   Original ROM size used on the Mac 128 and 512. Followed by 128 Kb ROM. See also *read-only memory (ROM)*.

128K ROM   Standard ROM on the Mac Plus, SE, and Mac 512 Kb enhanced. See also *read-only memory (ROM)*.

Accelerator board   An expansion card that, when installed in the Macintosh, enables the computer to operate and manipulate data at a faster rate.

Acoustic modem   A modem with two cups that fit around a telephone's handset; converts a computer's signals into sound and back again. See also *modem*.

Active window   The top or front window on the Desktop. It has a highlighted title bar.

Alert box   Contains a warning when you ask the Macintosh to do something that may cause loss of data, or when other errors occur. See also *dialog box*.

Alias   An icon that represents an original file folder or disk.

Apple Desktop Bus (ADB)   The connectors on the back of the Macintosh that allow connection of the keyboard, mouse, joysticks, graphics tablets, trackballs, and other input devices.

Apple HD SC Setup   A system utility program packaged with the Macintosh that initializes and sets up an Apple hard disk.

Apple key (or)   When pressed in combination with other keys, performs an action or command. Also known as the Command key or "cloverleaf" key.

Apple menu   The far left menu at the top of the Macintosh screen.

Apple menu items   Items available on the Apple menu of the Desktop for immediate use. These applications, folders, and files are placed in the Apple Menu Items folder.

AppleShare   An operating system designed to enable a Macintosh to become a server to other Macs on the same network.

AppleTalk   A communications network used to connect Macs and share peripheral devices such as printers. AppleTalk is the communication protocol by which data is transferred. Also called LocalTalk.

Application   A program that enables the user to create, enter, and design information. Examples are word processor, spreadsheet, and paint programs.

Arrow keys   The four keys that move the insertion point left, right, up, and down in a word processor file and change the active cell in a spreadsheet.

ASCII (American Standard Code for Information Interchange)   A standard computer text format in which each character is represented by seven bits. See also *text file*.

Asynchronous communication   A means of transmitting data between computers. A special signal indicates when each character starts and stops.

AV (AudioVisual)   A type of Apple video monitor that includes speakers and a microphone for improved quality of sound input and output.

Baud rate   A measure of speed equal to one signal per second. One baud represents one bit per second (bps). Common baud rates are 300, 1200, and 2400.

Bomb   An abnormal termination of a program. A bomb occurs when a program unexpectedly halts due to a bug or encounters data conditions it cannot handle.

Boot   To start a computer by loading the operating system (System file and Finder) into memory. The operating system software tells the Macintosh how to load other programs.

Buffer   A section of memory that temporarily holds information from I/O (input/output) communications, including data transfer through a modem, or reading and writing to your disk. The buffer holds information when the computer is sending information faster than the device can receive it.

Bundled software   Software included with your Macintosh, such as the System Tools disk, Utilities disk, and application software. Such a package deal includes hardware and software.

Bus   A path through which information is shared between one part of a computer and another.

Byte   A measure of the amount of information equivalent to the memory needed to store a character of the alphabet. 1,024 bytes equal 1 Kb of memory. A byte consists of eight bits and has eight 1s and 0s.

Cache A special section of RAM reserved for frequently used applications and utility information. Called the Disk Cache in the Memory control panel. See also *RAM cache.*

Caps Lock key A key located in the lower left corner of the Macintosh standard keyboard, or on the far left side of the Extended Keyboard, that, when pressed, causes alphabetic characters to be displayed in uppercase format but does not affect numeric keys or symbols.

Cathode-ray tube (CRT) The screen used in computers in which light produced by a electron gun strikes a phosphor coating on the screen.

CD-ROM drive A SCSI storage device that reads Compact Disc Read-Only Memory discs. These discs can hold up to 600 Mb of data, but data can only be read from them, not written to them.

Central processing unit (CPU) The computer's main information processing unit. In a Macintosh, the CPU is a single silicon chip called the microprocessor. See also *microprocessor.*

Chip A tiny piece of silicon with an integrated electronic circuit photoengraved on its surface.

Chooser A desk accessory that enables the user to choose the printer on which the document is to be printed. For the Chooser to function, the printer resource files must be installed in the current System file. In a networking environment, the Chooser can be used to connect and disconnect the Macintosh from the network and choose from among devices connected to the network.

Click To place the mouse pointer (arrow) on an item on-screen and quickly press and release the mouse button.

Clock speed The actual operating speed of the computer's microprocessor.

Close A command that closes a window or document.

Close box A small box located at the top left of a document window. Clicking the Close box causes the program to prompt the user to save the last changes to the document and to close the current window.

Cold boot Using the power switch to turn on your Macintosh.

Command A menu option that causes an action. A command tells the Macintosh what to do next.

Command key (⌘ and) See *Apple key.*

Control key A key located on the left side of the standard keyboard, or in the lower left corner of the Extended Keyboard, whose function varies depending upon the application being used.

Control Panel A desk accessory in System 6 that's used to personalize such features as the pattern on the Desktop, the speed of the mouse movement, and the volume of the warning beep.

Control Panels folder A folder in System 7 that resides in the System Folder and contains control panels. Replaces the Control Panel desk accessory of System 6.

Coprocessor A microchip that assists the main microprocessor with data-intensive tasks such as large spreadsheets, large databases, complex statistical analyses, or graphics activities.

Copy A command used to make an exact replica of a letter, an entire document, a graphic, an application, or even a disk. The Copy command is located in the Edit menu. Using Copy does not modify or delete the original.

Current startup disk The startup disk whose System files the Macintosh is using.

Cursor An icon indicating the current mouse location on-screen. The Macintosh has a variety of cursor shapes, including a vertical bar, I-beam, pointer, and wristwatch. See also *insertion point.*

Cut A command that removes selected information from a document and temporarily places it in the Clipboard.

Cylinder The total number of disk tracks that can be written or read for a specific disk-head position. On a double-sided floppy disk, a cylinder is two tracks; on a hard disk, it consists of four or more tracks. See also *track.*

DAT (digital audio tape) Used as a medium for data backup. A DAT cartridge can hold 2 Gb to 8 Gb of data.

Data The information processed with a computer application or program. Also called *information.*

Delete key A key that you press to remove information from a document. Using this key is the same as using the Cut command except that the information is not placed on the Clipboard; it is deleted permanently. See also *cut*.

Desktop   The work area of the Macintosh. The screen, disk icons, Trash can, and menu bar that you see when you start your Mac.

Dialog box   A message from the Macintosh requesting further action or information from the user. In most instances, the user may respond by typing a response or clicking a button. When accompanied by a beep, the user is being warned that something may happen that the user has not anticipated. See also *alert box*.

Direct-connect modem   A modem that connects directly from the computer into the telephone line outlet and bypasses the telephone handset.

Directory window   The window that lists the contents of a disk. On the Mac, disk directories are called folders. Using the View menu, the user can alter the appearance of the window and have the contents displayed in small icons, large icons, and words.

Disk   A device that uses magnetic medium to store information. Disks can be floppy or hard. The Macintosh uses 3.5-inch, hard-case floppy disks. A typical floppy disk can be single-sided (400 Kb), double-sided (800 Kb), or high density (1.4 Mb). Hard disk sizes can range up to 9 Gb.

Disk drive   Holds the disk and retrieves information stored on the disk. The user must insert a floppy disk into the floppy disk drive. A hard disk drive has a built-in disk permanently installed.

Disk drive port   A port on the Macintosh designed to be connected to an external floppy disk drive. See also *port*.

Document   A generic term describing whatever the user creates, using an application on the Macintosh. A document can be a letter, article, picture, table, or spreadsheet, among other things. A document contains the information the user has entered and saved.

Dot-matrix printer   A printer that forms characters and graphics from dots. The ImageWriter II is a dot-matrix printer.

Dots per inch (dpi)   A measure of screen and printer resolution by the number of dots per linear inch. The higher the number of dots, the better the resolution. The ImageWriter II operates at 144 dpi, and the LaserWriter operates at 300 dpi. See also *resolution*.

Double-click   An action used to open applications, documents, or folders. Double-clicking is performed by clicking the mouse button twice in rapid succession.

Download   A procedure in which a user transfers data from a remote computer's database to the user's computer and stores the data on a hard disk or floppy.

Dpi   See *dots per inch*.

Drag   A technique used to move icons from one location to another. The user places the mouse pointer on the icon, presses and holds down the mouse button, moves the pointer to where the icon should be, and then releases the mouse button.

Driver   Software that tells the Macintosh how to operate an external device such as a printer. A driver is located in the System Folder.

Edit menu   A menu that contains the copying and cutting features and the Undo command.

Electronic mail   See *e-mail*.

E-mail   A messaging system that enables the user to send and receive messages to people in and outside the user's computer network. Outside messages are generally sent using telephone lines. A message can be as simple as a quick note or as complex as multiple documents and files.

Emulation   A feature that enables one device to imitate another. Used on the Power Macintosh computers so that they can run software originally written for the 680X0-based Macs.

Enter key   A key that confirms an entry. Similar to the Return key.

Ethernet   A standard for local area network hardware.

Expansion card   An internal card that enables features to be added to the computer's processing capability, telecommunications capability, and so on.

Expansion slot   A location inside the Macintosh that allows the installation of an expansion card to perform additional functions.

Extension   A system program that extends the capabilities of System 7's features. See also *INIT*.

Field   A piece of data in a database record.

File   Information stored on disk. Also called a *document*.

File format   The set of instructions used to store information.

File server   A node on a network that has a disk drive, software, and processor that is available to all users. File-server software controls access to individual files, and multiuser software enables several users to access the same file simultaneously.

Finder   A file and memory management utility that keeps the Desktop organized, thus enabling users to find and open files or folders. The Finder must be in the System Folder for your Macintosh to operate properly.

Floppy disk   A removable secondary storage medium that uses a magnetically sensitive, flexible disk enclosed in a plastic envelope or case.

Folder   Holds related information in one location like the folders in an office file cabinet. A folder can contain files, other folders, graphics documents, or other information.

Font   A collection of letters, punctuation marks, numbers, and symbols that appear in the same typeface, style, and size. The Macintosh comes with a number of typefaces, such as Monaco, Chicago, and Geneva.

Freeware   Software shared without costs to the user, with the intention that the software be shared by others and distributed throughout a large network of users. See also *public domain software* and *shareware*.

Function key   A key that can be programmed to perform a particular function.

Get Info   A command on the File menu that provides the following information on a file or folder: locked or unlocked, creation date, modification dates, size, and user-entered notes.

Gigabyte (Gb)   Around one billion bytes (1,073,741,824 bytes) or 1,024 megabytes.

GUI (graphical user interface)   The way the Mac and the Mac user interact with each other. The GUI takes full advantage of graphics by using icons and the mouse.

Hard disk drive   A disk drive contained inside or residing outside the Macintosh. The drive contains permanently installed disks that hold much more information than a floppy disk does and retrieves information faster than a floppy drive.

Hardware   The physical parts of the Macintosh: the screen, keyboard, mouse, disk drives, casing, cables, and all the electronic mechanisms and boards inside the Macintosh. Hardware also includes other pieces of computer equipment, such as printers and modems.

Hayes-compatible modem   A modem that sets modes and features with the AT command set that was developed by Hayes Microcomputer Products.

Header   Text that is automatically printed at the top of each page. That portion of a Macintosh disk file containing the file's directory information such as name, type, and source.

Hierarchical File System (HFS)   A system that enables the user to organize information with folders. The user can organize applications, documents, and other folders within folders to create levels in a hierarchy. See also *Macintosh File System*.

Highlight   Usually means to select something so that it appears different from the surrounding information. When a piece of information is highlighted, the user can initiate a command to modify that information—for example, you highlight a word when you are ready to make it bold.

High-profile SIMM   An in-line memory module that, when installed, is not flush with the motherboard.

I-beam   The shape the mouse pointer takes when the user is entering information or editing text. The pointer resembles the uppercase letter *I*.

Icon   A graphic representation of a file, folder, disk, or command. A file is generally represented as a sheet of paper, for example, and a folder looks like a manila folder.

ImageWriter   The first dot-matrix printer designed specifically for use with the Macintosh.

Impact printer   A printer that forms characters by striking an inked ribbon against paper. See also *dot-matrix printer*.

Incremental backup   One of two types of backups in which only those files changed since the last backup are backed up.

INIT   A utility file (called an *extension* in System 7) located in the System Folder. After you place an INIT file in the System Folder and restart the Macintosh, the INIT file becomes active. See also *extension*.

Initialize   To prepare a disk to be used by the Macintosh. Generally, when you initialize a disk, the Macintosh structures the disk into sectors and tracks. After a disk has been initialized, the Macintosh can use it to save information to and retrieve information from. Also called formatting a disk.

Ink cartridge   The replaceable container of ink used by an inkjet printer.

Inkjet printer   A printer that forms characters by spraying tiny streams of ink onto paper.

Input device   A device (such as a mouse, keyboard, trackball, or graphics tablet) that inputs information into your Macintosh.

Insertion point   The location in a document where the user may insert something. The insertion point is selected by placing the mouse pointer where you want the insertion to occur and clicking once. A blinking I-beam then appears at that point. See also *cursor*.

Installer   A separate application used to install software on your hard disk.

Interface   An electronic link between different computer devices, such as the computer and a mouse. The point where two elements meet. The connecting point between the Macintosh and the ImageWriter II, for example, is an interface. An interface may exist between two pieces of hardware, two pieces of software, or a piece of hardware and a piece of software.

Internal modem   A modem installed into a computer slot. A modem that is built directly into the computer.

Kilobits per second (Kbps)   A measure of data transfer speed, in thousands of bits per second.

Kilobyte (Kb)   1,024 bytes. A common measure of file size. A typical double-spaced page is 1.5 Kb.

LAN   See *local area network*.

Laptop computer   A portable computer about the size of a small briefcase. Can be moved easily and accessed in any setting. Apple's line of laptops are the PowerBook series of Macs.

Laser printer   A printer that forms characters and graphics by moving a laser beam across a photoconductive drum. The printer then projects the image onto paper. Macintosh laser printers are called LaserWriters. See also *toner*.

Launch   The act of double-clicking an application to start it.

Local area network (LAN)   Computers linked with cables and software. The computers can share files and external devices such as printers and disk drives. Many offices are linked together with LANs to improve communication and efficiency.

LocalTalk   The hardware portion of Apple's LAN system used to connect Macs to LaserWriters and other Macs.

Logic board   The board inside the Macintosh responsible for organizing and executing instructions. Also called the motherboard.

Low-profile SIMM   An in-line memory module flush with the motherboard when installed.

Macintosh File System (MFS)   A method of organizing files and folders where folders cannot be nested within folders. Followed by the Hierarchical File System (HFS). See also *Hierarchical File System*.

Macintosh user group   An association of Macintosh enthusiasts of various levels of proficiency who meet to discuss issues relating to the Mac. User groups are located throughout the country. Many have a newsletter, which provides members with updated information and tips. You can find your local user group by calling Apple at 800-538-9696.

Megabyte (Mb)   A unit of measure representing 1,048,576 bytes (or 1,024 Kb) of storage capacity on a disk or in RAM. Hard disks are typically measured in terms of the amount of storage capacity. A 20 Mb hard disk indicates that the storage capacity of this disk drive is 20 Mb and will hold approximately 20,480 Kb of information.

Memory   The primary internal location within the computer where internal instructions are stored. The location in the Macintosh's central processing unit that holds information. Some of this memory is used by applications necessary to do complex calculations or sort data (RAM). Other memory is permanently used by the Macintosh and is not accessible to the user (ROM). See also *random-access memory (RAM)* and *read-only memory (ROM)*.

Menu   A list of commands available to the user. You can open a menu by clicking the menu's name at the top of the screen. The user holds down the mouse button, moves the mouse pointer down the list of menu commands, and then releases the mouse button on the command needed.

Menu bar   The top line on-screen. It horizontally lists the menus available to the Macintosh user. See also *menu*.

Microcomputer   A small, relatively inexpensive computer developed primarily for use by one person. Also referred to as a *personal computer* or *home computer*. A Macintosh is a microcomputer.

Microfloppy disk   A 3.5-inch flexible disk contained within a semi-rigid plastic casing. See also *floppy disk*.

Microprocessor   A small silicon chip containing a large number of electronic components. The microprocessor chip can operate on large amounts of information when used with other computer components.

Modem (modulator/demodulator)   A peripheral device that enables computers to communicate by telephone lines.

Monitor   The screen associated with a computer. The light-blue Macintosh Plus, SE, and Classic monitors are located directly above the disk drives, all contained in one cabinet. Other Macintoshes have a separate monitor, which is not enclosed with the CPU or disk drives. Monitors can be color or monochrome.

Motherboard   The main board (also called the logic board) in the Macintosh that contains the central processing chips, RAM, and expansion slots.

Mouse   A hand-held device used to navigate on the Macintosh screen. The mouse can be used to access the menus and select information. When you move the mouse, the pointer moves on-screen in the corresponding direction.

Mouse button   The button located on the mouse. By pressing the mouse button (clicking), an action is initiated. By releasing the button, the action is acknowledged.

Nanosecond (ns)   One billionth of a second.

Network   A computer communication pathway using hardware and software that links multiple computers and peripheral devices so that each computer or device shares information. See *node* and *local area network*.

Node   A device on a network (such as a computer, a hard disk, or a printer) that can send and receive information. See also *network*.

NuBus   A high-speed information pathway for modular Macs. You plug expansion cards into NuBus.

Null modem   A cable connecting two computers. Used for communication purposes rather than a modem.

Online help   A file contained within an application that can provide the user with help as the application continues.

Open   The act of accessing a document for changing or viewing.

Operating system   The System Software, which controls the functioning of the Macintosh and the direction of information flow among computer components. See also *System Software*.

Optical Character Recognition   A technology by which printed characters are optically scanned and translated into codes that the computer can process. The device that has this capability is known as an optical character reader (OCR) or scanner. See also *scanner*.

Optical disc   A disc on which music or data is recorded in the form of small pits. The data or music is retrieved with a laser beam.

Option key   A Macintosh key used with other keys to perform particular operations.

Parameter RAM   Memory devoted to certain system settings such as the time, date, and the alarm clock.

Partition   A physically separate section on a hard disk that can be used with the same or a different operating system.

Paste   A command that retrieves from the Clipboard a copied or cut piece of data and places the data at the insertion point in a document.

Path   The hierarchical path to a folder, application, or document file that reflects the organization of a particular group of information. A hard disk, for example, contains a folder called Folder 1, which contains a second folder called Folder 2. Within Folder 2 are three letters (Let1, Let2, Let3). To identify the path of Let3, you identify the name of the disk and progress toward document Let3 in this manner: Hard disk:Folder 1:Folder 2:Let3:.

Peripheral device   A unit of computer hardware such as a printer, modem, or external hard disk drive. Peripheral devices usually are connected to the Macintosh with cables.

Personal computer (PC)   A generic term used to describe a computer designed for use at home or in a small-business setting. In general, a Macintosh is not referred to as a PC, because the term has come to mean any IBM or IBM-compatible computer.

PICT   An object-oriented graphic format used to store MacDraw documents.

Pixel (picture element)   A single dot or picture element on the Macintosh display. A pixel is the visual representation of a bit in which a pixel is white if the bit is equal to 0 and black if the bit is equal to 1.

Platter   The glass or metal circular component of a hard disk that spins and on which data is written and from which data is read.

Pointer   An icon, usually arrow-shaped, that reflects the movement of the mouse.

Port   A connection socket on the back of the Macintosh that enables the user to connect a printer cable, hard disk drive, modem, keyboard, or mouse to the Macintosh.

PostScript   A page description programming language written by Adobe, Inc. to prepare an image for printing on a laser printer. PostScript fonts are used with PostScript-compatible printers. These fonts are widely recognized as the standard in near-typeset quality printing. Also called *encapsulated PostScript (EPS) format*.

Power Macintosh   Any of the Macintosh computers based on the PowerPC family of microprocessors.

Printer driver   The software containing the instructions that enable the computer to communicate with the printer.

Printer port   A serial port designed for the connection of a printer or modem to the computer. See also *serial port*.

Processor Direct Slot   A expansion plug on the motherboard of many Macintoshes. Used for high-speed, direct communication with the microprocessor.

Program   A set of instructions, usually in the form of a programming language, that tells a computer what to do.

Programmer's switch. A switch on the side of many Macintosh computers that enables you to reboot the computer and access the Macintosh's debugging utility.

Protocol   In computer telecommunications, the set of commands, rules, and procedures determining how information travels between computers.

Public domain software   Software that can be copied without copyright infringement. See also *shareware* and *freeware*.

Pull-down menu   A menu that appears only when accessed by the user. At all other times, only the menu titles are visible.

QuickDraw   A computer code that resides in the Macintosh's ROM and facilitates the generation of images for the screen and printer.

Radio button   A round button, found in dialog boxes, that you click to choose a particular option.

RAM   See also *random access memory*.

RAM cache   A portion of the RAM memory that can be designated to hold data that is used repeatedly by an application.

RAM disk   A program that sets aside part of the Macintosh's memory and programs the computer to recognize this memory as a disk drive.

Random-access memory (RAM)   The part of the Macintosh's memory that allows temporary storage of data. Because RAM is only temporary, any information left in RAM is lost when the computer is turned off.

Read-only memory (ROM)   The part of the Macintosh's memory that permanently stores System information and contains the information needed to start up. Also called firmware.

Reboot   The act of restarting the computer.

Removable media   Typically a cartridge containing magnetic media such as a disk or tape that can be removed from the computer's storage device.

Resolution   The number of dots per inch (dpi) displayed on a screen or a printed document. The Macintosh Plus and SE screens, for example, have a resolution of 72 dpi. The LaserWriter has a resolution of 300 dpi. See also *dots per inch.*

Restart   To reset a computer to its startup state without turning off the power. The Macintosh has two procedures for restart: a menu command and the programmer's switch. Also referred to as a *warm boot.*

Return key   The key, located on the right side of the main keyboard, that instructs the Macintosh to move the cursor to the next line. Similar to the *Enter key.*

ROM   See *read-only memory.*

Root directory   The first level of organization of the top level created when the disk is formatted.

Run   The act of executing a program or an application.

Save   A command instructing the Macintosh to store information on disk.

Save As   A command instructing the Macintosh to save the current document using a different name or file format, or on a different disk drive.

Scanner   A device used to capture graphics and text for use in Mac applications. See also *Optical Character Recognition.*

Scroll   A method of moving within a document. Using the scroll bars located on the right and bottom of the screen, the user can move forward, backward, left, and right to see other portions of the document. Scroll arrows, located in the scroll bars, move the document one line or column at a time in the direction desired. The user can scroll continuously through a document by clicking the arrow and holding the mouse button.

SCSI   See *Small Computer System Interface.*

SCSI chain   A group of cables and peripherals connected to an Apple computer.

SCSI ID   The address along the SCSI chain that serves to identify a particular SCSI device. SCSI ID's must be unique, in the range of 0–7.

SCSI port   A port located on the back of the Macintosh that enables the user to connect a SCSI cable from a peripheral device to the Macintosh.

Sector   On a disk, the smallest continuous physical space for saving data. Multiple sectors define a track. See also *track* and *cylinder.*

Select   An operation used to indicate where the next action should take place. To select an object, the user double-clicks the icon or word, or drags the mouse across the object.

Serial interface   A form of data transmission in which the bits of each character are transmitted sequentially one by one over a single channel or wire. The most common serial interface is the RS-232 cable and connector.

Serial port   A connector on the back of the Macintosh that enables the user to connect serial devices using a serial interface. See also *printer port.*

Server   On a network, any device or computer that all users can share.

Shareware   Copyrighted computer programs that users can try on a trial basis. If you like the software, you are expected to pay a fee to the program's author. See also *public domain software* and *freeware.*

Shutdown   The process of saving all work, closing all folders and files, ejecting all disks, and turning off the power of the computer.

SIMM (Single in-line memory module)   A memory module that plugs into the motherboard.

Slot   A location on an internal board where additional cards can fit.

Small Computer System Interface (SCSI)   A standard interface that enables the user to connect a peripheral device to the Macintosh.

Software   A generic term for computer programs. Software tells the computer hardware how to perform its work. Software can be categorized into many areas, including systems software, utility software, and applications software.

Startup disk   A disk that contains the System files the Macintosh needs to get started. A startup disk must contain the System file and Finder and generally contains printer resources and desk accessories. The startup disk is the first disk inserted into a floppy disk system. In a hard disk system, the startup disk is contained on the hard disk and automatically boots when the power switch is turned on. See also *boot.*

Startup screen   The opening screen containing words and graphics that appears when booting the Macintosh. Many utilities enable the user to customize the startup screen.

Suitcase   The icon that represents a set of fonts or desk accessories.

SyQuest   A removable-cartridge drive and cartridge storage system. Cartridges can be removed from the drive, allowing you to expand storage easily.

System 7.5   Apple's latest version of the Macintosh operating system.

System file   A file that contains information the Macintosh uses to operate and start up. System files cannot be opened in the usual manner but can be modified. The Macintosh cannot operate without a System file.

System Folder   The folder that contains the important System and Finder files necessary to boot up and run the Macintosh.

System Software   The files, extensions, control panels, utilities, desk accessories, fonts, and resources located in the System Folder as provided by Apple. This software is all the Macintosh needs to run properly. See also *operating system.*

System Tools disk   Software disks packaged with the Macintosh that provide the user with various tools to facilitate using the Macintosh.

Tape drive   A SCSI storage unit used for backing up and archiving data on tape media. Benefits include large capacity, good speed, and easy rotation of backup media for maximum data safety.

Telecommunications   Sharing information over phone lines through the use of a modem and telephone lines.

Terminator or SCSI terminator   A series of resistors that serve to cancel unwanted signals in and along the SCSI chain. A terminator must be placed at the end of an external chain of SCSI devices.

Text file   A computer file that contains sequences of bits that represent characters. Also known as an ASCII file. See also *ASCII.*

Title bar   The multilined bar at the top of the active window that displays the title of the document or window.

Toner   A black powder used in laser printers and photocopiers that serves as ink in the printing of characters and images. See also *laser printer.*

Toolbox   A collection of drawing and painting tools found in many applications such as HyperCard, MacDraw, and MacPaint.

Touch pad   A pointing device that is used by moving a finger over a receptive flat surface.

Track   A location on magnetic media that stores data. Tracks are concentric circles on the surface of a disk made up of sectors. One or more tracks make up a cylinder of disk space. See also *cylinder* and *sector.*

Trackball   A pointing device that essentially is an inverted mouse, in which the ball is located on top of the device. The user moves the ball rather than the device, which remains stationary. A pointed arrow on-screen reflects the ball's movement just as though a mouse is being used. See also *mouse.*

Tractor-feed printer   A printer that advances paper through the use of pins that fit into preformed holes on the edges of the computer paper.

Trash can   A storage location on the Desktop used to discard documents, folders, and applications. The Trash can is not emptied until the user selects Empty Trash from the Special menu, or until other disk operations are performed. If the Trash can has not been emptied, documents that have been trashed can be reclaimed by double-clicking the Trash can and retrieving the document. The retrieved document then must be placed back into the folder from which it originally came.

U **Upload** A procedure in which a user transfers information from his or her computer to a remote computer.

User group A group of people who have an interest in a particular computer or a particular type of application such as desktop publishing.

Utilities disk A disk packaged with the Macintosh that contains utilities used to maintain your computer system. Examples of utility programs contained on this disk are the Font/DA Mover and the Installer.

V **Video card** A circuit board containing the video controller and related components that connects into a computer to control the video display. See also *video controller circuit.*

Video controller circuit A circuit that modifies digital information to create the signal necessary for display on a computer screen. See also *cathode-ray tube (CRT).*

Video RAM A section of RAM devoted to screen information. In the Macintosh, the video RAM stores a bit-mapped image of the screen display. See also *random-access memory (RAM).*

Virtual memory The use of the available space on a hard disk to increase the RAM available for application use.

W **Warm boot** The act of selecting the Restart command on the Special menu so that the computer boots without turning the power off and on.

Window The area on the Desktop that displays information. To view a document, the user uses a window. Windows can be opened or closed, moved around on the Desktop, resized, and scrolled through.

Wristwatch cursor Appears on-screen when the Macintosh is busy performing some activity. During the time that the wristwatch is on the screen, the user cannot access additional commands. The wristwatch's hands turn, indicating that the Macintosh is working.

Write-protect tab A small tab or box built into a 3.5-inch disk casing to prevent accidental erasure or over-writing of disk contents.

Z **Zoom box** A box located on the right side of the title bar that the user clicks to expand the active window to its maximum size. By clicking the zoom box again, the user can return the window to its previous size.

Index

Symbols

A

B

C

D

U

V

W-Z